THE ROLE OF BRIEF THERAPY
IN ATTACHMENT DISORDERS

Other titles in the UKCP Series:

THE ROLE OF BRIEF THERAPY IN ATTACHMENT DISORDERS

Lisa Wake

On behalf of the United Kingdom Council
for Psychotherapy

with contributions and Foreword by Betty Alice Erickson

KARNAC

First published in 2010 by
Karnac Books Ltd
118 Finchley Road, London NW3 5HT

British Library Cataloguing in Publication Data

A C.I.P. for this book is available from the British Library

ISBN: 978 1 85575 697 7

Edited, designed and produced by The Studio Publishing Services Ltd
www.publishingservicesuk.co.uk
e-mail: studio@publishingservicesuk.co.uk

www.karnacbooks.com

CONTENTS

CHAPTER FIVE
Outcome orientation as a model of psychotherapy

CHAPTER SIX
The therapist's role in brief therapy

CHAPTER SEVEN
Conclusions

REFERENCES

INDEX

ACKNOWLEDGEMENTS

I am grateful to my clients, students, teachers and peers for their feedback and contributions to this work. All client case material is anonymous to maintain the confidentiality of their work and is printed with full permission of the client.

Specific acknowledgements are paid to:

Betty Alice Erickson, whose contribution, feedback, and Foreword has enabled me to make a greater connection to the work of her father, Milton Erickson. Erickson has long been of influence in my work and it has been an honour to work so closely with Betty Alice as my thinking has developed.

Steve Gilligan, for his willingness to critique my understanding of his work and permission to include this.

The Association for Cognitive and Analytic Therapy: colleagues who have responded in a timely manner to my requests for information and who have been very open in enabling me to include elements of research from a therapy that I have little knowledge of. Their holistic approach to their work with clients with a history of borderline processes can only bring a much-needed dimension to the role of the therapeutic relationship within complex processes.

Nick Kemp and his "non-provocative" critique of my understanding of Frank Farrelly's work in provocative therapy.

Harvey Ratner at BRIEF for his enduring persistence in ensuring that I fully represented solution focused brief therapy in an appropriate and respectful way. Also to Mike Roarty, who helped me put aside my own model and prejudices and begin to gain greater understanding of SFBT.

Therapists Franca Mongiardi, Mark Wake, and Ann Hunter for painstakingly critiquing and editing my work as it progressed.

Pippa Weitz at Karnac for holding the space while I moved through my own process of doubt.

Finally, and most importantly, to my clients, who have taken a significant step in their own lives and who have honestly and earnestly considered the inclusion of their work and process in this book. I have learnt much from working with each of you.

Lisa is a highly experienced and well respected psychotherapist, trainer, coach, facilitator, and change management consultant.

After starting her career in National Health Service (NHS) clinical practice as a nurse, Lisa moved into NHS management in 1992, where she was employed as a senior manager until she left to commence her own shared business in 1997. Using neurolinguistic programming (NLP) as a launch pad, Lisa has developed extensive experience as a coach, facilitator, change agent, trainer, supervisor, and mentor. Now a Master Trainer of NLP, Lisa is accredited by the UK Council for Psychotherapy as a neurolinguistic psychotherapist. She has a BSc (Hons) in Professional Studies in Health Care and a MSc in Advanced Clinical Practice, and has undertaken a range of further career-associated trainings.

As a psychotherapist, Lisa has served as both Chair and Vice Chair of the UKCP, working closely with the government on the statutory regulation of psychology, psychotherapy, and counselling, and has long been a proponent of the effectiveness of brief therapy. She has actively campaigned for rigour of standards, ethics, and research in psychotherapy, and has contributed to the neurolinguistic psychotherapy field with the publication of her ground-breaking book for the Advancing Theory in Therapy series for Routledge, *Neurolinguistic Psychotherapy: A Postmodern Perspective* (2008). Lisa continues to support UKCP and is on the editorial board for the Karnac UKCP series.

Lisa was instrumental in working with the government and Department of Health on the statutory regulation of psychotherapy and the White Paper on the regulation of non-medical professionals. She worked closely with Skills for Health in implementing the groundwork for the development of National Occupational Standards for Psychotherapy. She also challenged the notion of a therapeutic monoculture for psychotherapy and provided researched-based evidence within the Department of Health and House of Lords to counter the drive by the Department of Health to exclude equally effective forms of psychotherapy.

Lisa parallels her psychotherapy practice with her consultancy work with a wide range of organizations, and is currently researching the effectiveness and application of NLP in corporate environments. She has an established portfolio of clients in the public and commercial sectors, including Northern Foods Group, BASF, Napp Pharmaceuticals, Mundipharma Research and Development, Telford and Wrekin Council, Tees, Esk and Wear Valleys NHS Trust, Cardiff and Vale NHS Trust, and Communities First Cardiff.

Lisa's most significant project in the commercial sector is to work as management development consultant to Northern Foods since 2000. She has assisted the organization to manage a changing agenda within the Northern Foods Group and to increase their market share of quality products. Within the public sector, Lisa has worked closely with the NHS Modernisation Agency in implementing the national Clinical Governance Framework for medical and pharmacy contracts.

Lisa acts as adviser to ANLP International, an umbrella body for supporting NLP in the UK, providing clinical and specialist support to the organization. She was also co-opted on to the steering group of the first International NLP conference.

In addition to the book *Neurolinguistic Psychotherapy*, Lisa has published a number of articles on neurolinguistic programming and psychotherapy.

Combining an active business consultancy, research, and writing career, Lisa balances her working life with an attempt at "the good life" with her husband and business partner, Mark. They breed and keep chickens, and grow most of their own produce, which is then used to cater for their own in-house training programmes.

FOREWORD

The Role of Brief Therapy in Attachment Disorders is a treasure! It combines the best of a clearly organized and valuable reference book with the air of a highly readable basic book. An examination of various treatment modalities for any disorder is a formidable task. To do this for attachment disorder, which does not have an enormous amount of literature surrounding it, is even more daunting. Lisa Wake takes a logical, step-by-step approach to accomplish this; she is painstaking, covers an enormous amount of material, yet she never bores the reader. Even in the midst of a highly researched chapter, the reader is amazed at how much detailed material is given in interesting and readily comprehensible ways.

One of Wake's goals is supporting the effectiveness of the often more popular brief therapies, including NLPt, for attachment disorder treatment. Short-term therapy is important, not only for humanitarian reasons, but because economics and limited resources are requiring it more and more. However, we all want high quality, and she wants to show, and does show, that high quality is an integral part of brief therapy treatment for attachment disorders.

She starts by describing many of the major brief therapies, noting how much research supports their efficacy. Then she does the same with some of the more traditional, analytically-based therapies. All these descriptions are well-researched and meticulously cited. To make her job even more complex, she then adds material gleaned from some of the latest research in neuroscience and from studies of the developing and psychologically traumatized brains, especially those of infants.

Last, but far from least, in order to support the value and usefulness of brief therapies, or of any therapy, she has to include research-based studies for them all. So she does. Even though some of the brief therapies have few research studies supporting their value, this lack, thankfully, does not prevent their inclusion. She also mentions that brief therapies often have individualized components. This individualization, especially of interventions, is beneficial to clients. However, it creates difficulties in providing valid research studies. This may be one of the reasons that research is difficult to find.

Wake does all these complicated and complex comparisons and contrasts with ease. Further, and more impressively, she achieves it without creating the unpleasant situation of the reader wanting the book to end. Not only is attention held, but one wishes there were more to read.

In her descriptions of many varied therapies, Wake sometimes quotes other therapists. This avoids the trap of her own interpretation skewing the explanations, and provides nice counterpoints to her style of writing. Those quotes are then tied to definitions of attachment disorders.

While discussing outcomes for the various therapies, Wake adds brain research about the effects of stress and arousal on the nervous systems. The mother's responses to the infant's arousal are critical for proper brain development. When that does not happen, the infant's brain does not learn crucial tasks. Wake then forms a neat connection to attachment disorder, including numerous and appropriate citations.

Once that is done, off she goes! Again, she makes complex concepts packed with dense information interesting. She ties together early experiences of stress and arousal without proper nurturing and the resulting problems for the child's ability to process various stimuli. This leads to the older child, the adult even, having unconscious motivations for, and reasons to keep, problematic behaviours. Then therapy is needed. The most efficient therapy, she writes, is to learn to process and to experience processing through the right brain. The therapies that work primarily with the somatic self, the unconscious, with the right brain, are primarily brief therapies. Working with the unconscious, the right brain, they help to repair the neural damage caused by the early harm to the infant's ability to self- regulate. The therapies that include right-brain activity as a part of their protocol are efficient. They help the patient to learn unlearnt abilities, re-learn poorly learnt responses, almost by re-experiencing and by processing in the unconscious, in the right brain. The reader is left thinking, "I knew all that, I just didn't have the words for it, let alone such neat and concise wording."

The last two chapters emphasize the significance of this notion. More significantly, they also give unambiguous information about the importance of the therapist's behaviours and orientation in the therapeutic situation. The connection between the therapist and the patient, and the therapist's unconscious and the patient's unconscious, is discussed and interwoven with this seminal idea. Citations abound here as Wake shows that several brief therapies have long focused on this. She has twenty topic headings, and supports them all.

Even with her belief in the power of well-done brief therapies, Wake finishes her summary with a sincere tribute to the other types of therapies. They are all useful, but the obvious conclusion is that some are more useful than others.

Scattered throughout the book are gems that break any possible heaviness in her well-researched facts. Wake includes case histories, with clear explanations of what happened and why things worked.

Also throughout the book are a number of figures and tables. These are all easy to read, and easier to understand. They not only summarize her major points, they provide a very useful resource for the reader. They are almost "cheat-sheets" to define various therapies. The figures and tables alone are well worth the purchase of the book.

Her book concludes with a famous quotation from my father Milton Erickson: "Into each life some confusion should come . . . and also some enlightenment". Lisa Wake has taken that to heart.

In *The Role of Brief Therapy in Attachment Disorders*, she has taken some confusion about various therapies and treatments of attachment disorder, and given some enlightenment.

Betty Alice Erickson, MS, LMFT
Dallas, Texas

CHAPTER ONE

The purpose of the book

W ithin the brief therapy field, there is a plethora of books on the "how to" of each approach, most of which are effective at demonstrating the approach. Many of the therapists who are recognized within the brief therapy field originated from psychodynamic or systemic schools, having moved across to what they identify as briefer, more respectful, outcome-orientated approaches. Only a few of the publications in this arena are underpinned by theory, research, and evidence-based practice, yet the therapies appear to work.

With the increasing understanding of neuroscience and developmental theory, there is now the opportunity to make the links between these therapies and those that are grounded in a more psychodynamic approach, specifically for attachment disorder and related problems. By adding to the understanding that exists in the field, and supporting this through grounded research, brief therapy may then take its place as a therapy equal to those that have been long recognized in the psychodynamic world.

As the field of knowledge continues to grow in neuroscience, there are inevitably implications which arise for psychotherapy, particularly when there are increasing pressures on the public sector to provide psychological interventions that are effective and yet are delivered in the briefest time frame possible.

This book aims to provide students, therapists, educators, and individuals interested in furthering the field of psychotherapy with an opportunity to review brief therapy in relation to attachment disorders in the light of what is becoming known in neuroscience.

In this first chapter, I provide an overview of brief therapy in the twenty-first century and a summary of the main brief therapies. Each of these therapies is explained in the context of definition, working principles, and evidence base. In considering the evidence base, I have used the guidelines from the Critical Appraisal Skills Programme (CASP, 1999, 2006) analysis as the basis for inclusion of research studies. I have also focused on studies that are included in the Cochrane Study of Systematic Reviews. This chapter tabulates the existing evidence base for each therapy in treating attachment and related disorders.

Chapter Two includes an integration of the current understanding within outcome orientated and brief therapies, of core belief structures, and the theories of object relations and attachment disorder. Also included is an abstract from a qualitative research study into the relationship between the core belief structures of NLPt (neurolinguistic psychotherapy) and object relations theory.

The neuroscientific theories of Schore, Gerhardt, and Hart are considered in Chapter Three and linked to attachment theory and MacLean's triune brain. A case study example is given to demonstrate the impact that neurological deficits arising from attachment disorders can have on subsequent relationships.

Continuing from Chapter Three, creating potential for repair and neurological growth is discussed across the brief therapies in Chapter Four. The chapter concludes with a consideration of Erickson's work with anxiety disorders in children and case studies of this work in action.

The principle processes of the outcome-orientated nature of the psychotherapies discussed in this first chapter are considered in Chapter Five. Integrated with this is the more recent understanding in neuroscience of attachment problems in relation to stress and arousal responses. The processes of goal orientation and outcomes are discussed, and a review of the outcome process of each therapy is completed. Stress and arousal responses are discussed, followed by underpinning theories on goal activation. Two goal-setting processes, NLP (neurolinguistic programming) and SFBT (solution focused brief therapy) are described. This is supported by summaries of techniques that enable visualization and accessing of associated states, including triggered responses.

The role of the therapist is considered, alongside the recent research into mirror neurons and how these may be activated within the therapeutic process, in Chapter Six. A series of case studies describe how this has worked in therapy.

The book concludes with a review of existing psychotherapy research into this area, and recommendations for ongoing clinical practice.

The position of brief therapy in the twenty-first century

There is an increasing burden on the National Health Service (NHS) and the Department of Work and Pensions from those individuals who are unable to work because of mental illness. The Depression Report (Layard et al., 2006) identified in up to 50% of all people in receipt of incapacity benefit that this is due to mental illness as either a primary or secondary factor. There are also increasing pressures on the NHS to provide effective treatments that are evidence based. Currently cognitive–behavioural therapy (CBT) is the preferred treatment of choice, identified by the National Institute for Clinical Excellence (NICE) (2004a) because of its brevity and demonstrable effectiveness through randomized controlled trials (RCT). This is the Department of Health's (DoH) gold standard for the assessment and evaluation of acceptable models of treatment. There are no NICE guidelines for attachment disorder. The guidelines for eating disorders (2004b), obsessive–compulsive disorder (2005), depression (2007a) and anxiety (2007b) all recommend CBT. The depression guidelines recommend "psychological treatment, specifically focused on depression (such as problem-solving therapy, brief CBT and counselling)", (p. 7), and "interpersonal therapy" (p. 17). However, the guidelines go on to highlight, "where patient preference or clinical opinion favours the use of Interpersonal Therapy, it may be appropriate to draw the patient's attention to the more limited evidence base for this therapy" (p. 29).

Where patients have atypical depression, "a longstanding pattern of interpersonal rejection and oversensitivity" (p. 31), the treatment of choice is to prescribe SSRIs (selective serotonin re-uptake inhibitors).

The NICE guidelines identify CBT as the preferred treatment of choice, as this is the only modality of psychological therapy that has an evidence base for effectiveness using randomized control trials (Dobson, 1989; Hollon & Beck 2004; Hollon, Thase & Markowitz, 2002; Westbrook & Kirk, 2005). Yet, research conducted by Stiles, Barkham, Twigg, Mellor-Clark, and Cooper (2006) demonstrates that theoretically different psychotherapy approaches tend to have equivalent outcomes. Hamer and Collinson (1999) suggest that there are a number of factors that influence this drive towards evidence based practice within the health service, not least those of cost pressures. CBT is a brief model of psychotherapy that typically lasts between six and twenty sessions, therefore fulfilling the Department of Health's aim of providing brief psychotherapeutic interventions at limited cost. Within the wider field of psycho-therapy, most other approaches require a prolonged time in therapy, often between one and five years. Yet, there are other psychotherapy approaches closely related to CBT, such as the brief therapies, which, if proved effective, would fulfil a realistic economic aim of effective psychotherapy that is brief and time limited.

The next section within this chapter reviews each of the brief therapies, providing a brief description and summarizing the work-ing principles and evidence base. Where possible, I have validated each of the sections with the most relevant association representing the therapy.

Cognitive analytic therapy

Cognitive analytic therapy (CAT) (Ryle, 1990, 1995a) is an inte-grated model of psychotherapy that is underpinned by object rela-tions theory and Kelly's personal construct theory. It also links to psychological theories within cognitive–behavioural therapy, although it does not limit itself to the more behavioural aspects of a client's presentation. As CAT has developed since the early 1990s, it has focused specifically on working with clients with personality disorders, mainly borderline personality disorder. Ryle's theory considers that in early development of the personality, reciprocal roles are internalized. These roles are threefold, the self, the other, and the relationship between the self and other. When the client adopts a particular role, their partner will experience pressure to adopt the reciprocal role, for example, victim–bully. Some reciprocal role-playing may be seen as benign and functional, for example, care giver–care receiver, whereas others are seen as dysfunctional roles, for example, abuser–abused.

Working principles of cognitive analytic therapy

The aim of CAT is to enable clients to understand and manage self-limiting beliefs and emotional states by identifying, working with, and changing these patterns of expression. Similar, in ways, to cognitive–behavioural therapy, the client is supported to recognize the patterns which have developed as a series of coping mechanisms, and, through structured tasking, is encouraged to develop insight and different ways of responding. The role of the therapist within CAT is non-collusional, with the therapist working through any re-enactments that the client brings into the therapy.

The theoretical approach of CAT is referred to as the three "R's": reformulation, recognition, and revision. These steps are included within a psychotherapy file that acts as a workbook that the client can utilize between sessions. The therapist will present the client with their own observation of the presenting patterns and a reformulation of the problems as target areas to work on.

Reformulation is a process of narrative understanding that enables the client to script out patterns of interaction from past, present, and future relationships and to reformulate these in a more useful way. The process includes the transference and counter-transference relationships and addresses both interpersonal and intrapsychic processes.

Recognition enables the client to understand their previous patterns within a wider psychological frame, leading to the client gaining control over them.

Revision enables the identification and change of procedures that are considered to be ineffective. This is done through the shared understanding of the therapist and the client.

Evidence base for cognitive analytic therapy

There is evidence for the effectiveness of CAT within a single case study approach for clients with borderline personality disorder (Ryle, 1995b; Ryle & Beard, 1993).

The SPeDi (Sheffield Personality Disorders) trial (2007) is conducting a limited RCT with ten patients and comparing a team-based approach to care and standard psychological therapy. Kellet, Bennett, and Ryle (2009) have conducted a multi-site hermeneutic single case approach to routine care of patients with BPD in the NHS. The study looked at the application of CAT principles for both patients and staff who are involved with their care, particularly as the patients' role enactments in borderline personality disorder often have a direct impact on the staff caring for them. Measurements used for the patient group were the core outcome measure and the work and social adjustment scale. Staff measurements were the service engagement scale, and the team climate inventory. Collaboration improved over time in the patient group and there was no significant difference in the other scales. Of the staff elements of the study, 88% of staff felt that they had gained a more in-depth understanding of their clients and a greater awareness of the relationship with the patient; 75% felt that team cover had improved and level of risk reduced. CAT informed supervision was effective in improving clinical practice and the most significant improvement was in the way the team worked. Positive changes were also reported in client relationships. Early findings of this study are available, and it is anticipated that full results will be available via ACAT (Association for Cognitive Analytic Therapy).

Llewelyn (2009) has conducted a process study evaluating the Bennett, Parry, and Ryle (2006) model of rupture repair in CAT, using an adolescent sample. This study demonstrated that the therapist's ability to competently resolve ruptures using this model as a process measure could predict outcome.

Cognitive–behavioural therapy

Cognitive–behavioural therapy began its early history in behaviourism and the notion that cognitions are behaviours in their own right and can be altered, initially through changing conditioned responses (Pavlov, 1927; Skinner, 1961) and by using social learning theory (Bandura, 1977). Two former analysts developed this work, Ellis (1962), who developed rational emotive therapy, and Beck (1963, 1976; Beck, Shaw, Rush, & Emery, 1979), who developed what later became known as cognitive–behavioural therapy.

CBT is one of the most widely researched methods of psychological therapy and, as such, holds a high degree of credibility in scientific and medical environments (Roth & Fonagy, 2005). Evidence of the effectiveness of CBT extends beyond the government's focus on the RCT, with research conducted in a range of qualitative and quantitative methodologies, including case series, diary studies, service user reports, and practice based evidence (Mansell, in House & Loewenthal, 2008, p. 19).

Working principles of CBT

CBT is based in science and behavioural psychology. CBT is defined as a therapy "variously used to refer to behaviour therapy, cognitive therapy and to therapy based on the pragmatic combination of principles of behavioural and cognitive theories (BABCP)", (Mansell, in House & Loewenthal, 2008, p. 21). Therapists work closely with clients to enable clients to understand the relationship between thoughts, feelings, and behaviour. The focus is different from the more traditional approaches in psychotherapy, in that the client is encouraged to concentrate on the conscious experience of meaning making and the here and now representation of problems, rather than consider links to past problems and experiences. The therapy is time limited and involves clear strategies, goals, and timescales for developing psychological and/or behavioural skills. The focus is on enabling the client to work with their existing resources and there is a strong emphasis on the client continuing their therapeutic progress with "homework".

Grazebrook, Garland, and the Board of BABCP (2005) summarize the key major components in CBT as:

1.   The cognitive components—how people think about and give meaning to their situations and then go on to develop beliefs about themselves and their world. Cognitive interventions include guided discovery where clients are encouraged to find

alternative meanings and ways of thinking about situations. The client is then encouraged to test out these new interpretations which results in new ways of thinking and acting leading to a more balanced perspective on life.

2. The behavioural components—involve how people respond when distressed. CBT looks at assisting the client develop ways to face their underlying fears and test out assumptions that they may have developed in response to their fear, resulting in a change in behaviour as they realize that many of their fears are unfounded.

They also list the key factors that influence the effective delivery of CBT.

●   Therapeutic relationship.
●   Collaboration between the therapist and client where the client remains in charge of finding their own solutions.
●   Formulation of possible hypothesis of the presenting problem based on assessment and evidence based practice.
●   Socratic dialogue to probe for meanings and alternative ideas.
●   Homework, where the client puts into practice what they have learnt in sessions.

Evidence base for CBT

As highlighted earlier in this chapter, there is a strong drive towards the development of CBT as the preferred treatment of choice within the NHS. CBT has been very effective in responding to the calls for an evidence base for the treatment approach and has been equally effective in demonstrating this through the perceived "gold standard" for research-based evidence: the randomized control trial (RCT). A substantial number of RCTs have demonstrated that CBT is superior to, and equally as effective as, medication in the treatment of depressive and anxiety disorders (Clark et al., 1998, 2003, 2006; Davidson et al., 2004; Heimberg et al., 1990, 1998; Ost, 1996; Ost, Fellenius, & Sterner, 1991; Thom, Sartory, & Johren, 2000; Visser & Bouman, 2001; Warwick, Clark, & Cobb, 1996).

There is also evidence of the longitudinal benefits of CBT in this group of patients (Clark et al., 1994, 1999, 2003, 2006; Dugas et al.,

2003; Ehlers et al., 2003; Ehlers, Clark, Hackmann, McManus, & Fennell, 2005; Ladouceur et al., 2000; Ost, 1996).

Trials have also demonstrated that CBT is effective in group work for generalized anxiety disorder (Dugas et al., 2003), obsessive–compulsive disorder (MacLean et al., 2001), social phobia (Heimberg et al., 1998), and depression (McDermut, Miller, & Brown, 2001). Studies have demonstrated that individual therapy is more effective than group therapy for clients with depressive illness (Churchill et al., 2001). In clients with anxiety disorder, the behavioural element of CBT is equally effective in groups and individuals (Fals-Stewart, Marks, & Schafer, 1993; Heimberg et al., 1998; MacLean et al., 2001), whereas more complex treatments are less effective in groups (Mortberg, Clark, Sundin, & Aberg Wistedt, 2007; Stangier, Heidenreich, Peitz, Lauterbach, & Clark, 2003; Whittal, Thordarson, & MacLean, 2005).

There is an increasing push towards computerized CBT (CCBT), which has demonstrated that effect size is similar to that of self help (Kaltenthaler et al., 2006). It is proved to be less effective than therapist-delivered CBT (Ladouceur et al., 2000), with clients reporting less satisfaction with the approach than therapies with therapist involvement (Cavanagh & Shapiro, 2004; Rogers, Oliver, Bower, Lovell, & Richards, 2004). Evidence demonstrates that CCBT is not superior to non treatment in mild to moderate depression (Andersson et al., 2005; Christensen, Griffiths, & Jorm, 20004); PTSD (Lange et al., 2003), and panic disorder (Carlbring, Westling, Ljungstrand, Ekselius, & Andersson, 2001). Similar findings also exist for non-facilitator guided self help (Anderson et al., 2005; Hirai & Clum, 2006).

Whitfield and Williams (2003) summarize the evidence base for CBT in treating depression in busy clinical settings. The paper reviews the wide-ranging evidence base for CBT and also provides evidence for CBT compared to other therapies. The paper is specifically designed to review the case for CBT in a busy clinical setting and to reduce the amount of clinical time required for patients, recommending self-help processes as a suitable alternative to psychotherapy. Paykel, Scott, and Teasdale (1999) and Scott, Teasdale, and Paykel (2000) have demonstrated the effectiveness of CBT for patients with residual symptoms of depression following a major depressive episode, and a considerable reduction in relapse compared to the control group.

Siqueland, Rynn, and Diamond (2005) have conducted two studies of modified combination CBT and attachment-based family therapy with adolescents presenting with a primary diagnosis of generalized anxiety disorder (GAD) and separation anxiety disorder (SAD). Results demonstrated a reduction in symptoms based on therapist's evaluation and self-reported scores with no significant difference between treatments.

Eye movement desensitization and reprocessing (EMDR)

EMDR was developed by Shapiro after she discovered that eye movements appeared to decrease the amount of negative emotions she was experiencing at the time. She presented the results of a randomized controlled trial of the methodology with a group of post traumatic stress disorder (PTSD) sufferers (Shapiro, 1989). She developed this work further, and, by including other components, such as certain cognitive elements that enable reprocessing of memories, she developed what is now known as EMDR.

EMDR was specifically designed to treat traumatic memories, and, although it is now used to treat other anxiety related disorders, it is predominantly recognized for its effectiveness in treating PTSD, for which it has NICE approval.

Working principles of EMDR

EMDR is based on the principle that all information is stored within the physiological system of the body. Memories are linked within neural networks that contain the associated thoughts, images, emotions, and sensations, and it is possible to create new learning and associations with information that is already stored within the physiological system. Shapiro considers that when a traumatic memory or event occurs, the information processing remains incomplete, either because of the strong feelings that the memory generates or because of dissociation during the event itself. This process prevents the person from connecting to more resourceful ways of responding held within other physiological networks. Any subsequent event that reminds the client of the original event results in the reliving of the event resulting in PTSD. Shapiro considers that this also happens with events that may be considered minor resulting in dysfunctional reactions.

EMDR consists of five components that work with cognitive, affective, and somatic components of memory (Shapiro, 2001).

- Linking of memory components, where the client focuses on the image of the event, the associated negative belief and the resulting physical sensations. This process enables the formation of the initial connections to aid information processing.
- Mindfulness, where clients are asked to "notice" and to "let whatever happens, happen". It is this stabilized observer stance that facilitates the emotional processing proposed by Teasdale (1999).
- Free association: clients are asked to report on any new associations, insights, emotions, memories, images, or sensations that arise during the session. It is this free association that is thought to create associative links between the original trauma and other related experiences that enable processing of the traumatic material.
- Repeated access and dismissal of traumatic imagery: it is the repeated processing of the material that enables the client to achieve mastery and control of the negative images and stimuli.
- Eye movements and other dual attention stimuli, including hand tapping and auditory stimuli. Eye movements are thought to have a role in processing cognitive stimuli (Antrobus, Antrobus, & Singer, 1964).

Evidence base for EMDR

A number of meta-analyses have been conducted into the effectiveness of EMDR as a psychological intervention. Van Etten and Taylor's (1998) meta-analysis of forty-one studies and sixty-one outcome trials of the comparative efficacy of treatments for PTSD included interventions of drug therapy, behaviour therapy, EMDR, relaxation training, hypnotherapy, and dynamic therapy. Patients had chronic PTSD, according to the *Diagnostic and Statistical Manual of Mental Disorders* (*DSM*) *III, III-R,* and *IV* criteria. Comprehensive outcome measures were assessed and the authors concluded that the meta-analysis supports the use of behaviour therapy, EMDR, and SSRIs.

Shepherd, Stein, and Milne (2000) reviewed randomized controlled trials of EMDR in the treatment of PTSD, comparing the approach with no treatment and alternative psychotherapy treatments. Patients with certain psychological conditions were excluded from the studies, as were those who had previously received EMDR or CBT. The authors concluded that there is evidence to support EMDR; however, the evidence is of limited quality, recommending further research into this area, including longer follow-up research.

This was followed by a Cochrane systematic review of randomized controlled trials of the psychological treatment of PTSD (Bisson & Andrew, 2007). The review considered all types of intervention and included adults who had suffered from traumatic stress symptoms for three months or more. Outcome measures included the severity of clinician-rated stress symptoms, self-reported traumatic stress symptoms, depressive and anxiety symptoms, adverse effects, and drop-outs. The main conclusions of the review demonstrated that there was evidence that individual trauma focused CBT, EMDR, stress management, and group trauma focused CBT are effective in the treatment of PTSD. Other non-trauma focused psychological treatments did not demonstrate a reduction in symptoms. The authors noted that there was unexplained heterogeneity within the comparisons and that there is need for caution in considering the findings of the review.

Shapiro's work has been embraced by trauma therapists who work specifically with attachment-related problems, and the further work by van der Kolk (2005) has continued to contribute to EMDR as an effective therapy in attachment-based trauma. Shapiro (2002) and Madrid, Skolek, and Shapiro (2006) demonstrated that EMDR may be an appropriate treatment for bonding difficulties. Soberman, Greenwald, and Rule (2002) were able to demonstrate that EMDR was effective in reducing memory-related distress and problem behaviours in boys with conduct problems. Moses (2007) has included a comprehensive chapter on the integration of EMDR in conjoint therapy, specifically related to attachment issues. His summary proposes that using EMDR in couples therapy enables a deep and productive experience where couples are able to rapidly process interrelated attachment issues.

Ericksonian therapy

Ericksonian therapy is based on the work of psychiatrist and hypnotherapist Milton H. Erickson. Erickson's early therapeutic work as a psychiatrist provided a traditional and analytic view to psychotherapy; however, by the 1950s, his work evolved and he began to view symptoms as unconscious communication of desired growth and change. He viewed each client as unique, with a unique problem and a unique solution (Erickson & Keeney, 2006). He believed that each client and each problem is best treated with therapy crafted specifically for them, even though there are common themes. He is often remembered as using primarily indirect suggestions to the client's unconscious mind to create changes by using the person's own resources. In that way, healing occurred from within the client's system, and the client was often not consciously aware of why he was making changes. Therefore, he had to "take credit" himself, which enhanced his independence. What is frequently less recalled is that Erickson had no hesitation in being very direct and forceful if he deemed that was the most useful approach.

Working principles of Ericksonian therapy

The main principles of Ericksonian therapy can be defined as consisting of six core strategies (Short, Erickson, & Erickson Klein, 2005).

- Distraction, whereby the therapist creates opportunities for progress that appears to be unintentional to the conscious mind of the client. Erickson sometimes referred to this as "getting the patient to do something they want to do, but ordinarily would not" (*ibid.*, p. 41).
- Partitioning, where a previously perceived intolerable problem is broken down into smaller, more manageable parts.
- Progression leads on from partitioning. Once a client has partitioned elements of the problem into smaller and more manageable segments, it is then possible to create movement and change within the segment. This gives hope that the problem can be overcome, albeit in small amounts and initially only partially.
- Suggestion that change is possible, with suggestion being offered as both direct hypnotic processes and also through more conversational suggestions. Additionally, Erickson was a

master at the use of conversational or naturalistic hypnotic trance, where suggestions would be heard primarily by the unconscious.

- Reorientation that provides the client with an alternative perspective that enables the client to review their past, present, and future differently and gain hope of a more positive and purposeful future.
- Utilization of the more negative, shameful aspects of the self. The therapist acknowledges and positively recognizes these components of the client, enabling validation of the client's experience and sense of self. Sometimes, a change in emphasis or definition of these more negative aspects leads to a higher level of self-acceptance and healing.

Evidence base for Ericksonian therapy

There is limited research evidence for Ericksonian therapy. Simpkins and Simpkins (2008) conducted an exploratory outcome comparison between Ericksonian approaches to therapy and brief dynamic therapy. The study used comparative pre and post tests, using Clark Personal and Social Adjustment Scale (CPSAS), Hopkins Symptom Checklist (HSCL), Target Complaint (TC) and Global Improvement (GI) with clients attending six therapy sessions. No statistical differences were found, except on HSCL, where Ericksonian therapy was found to be more effective. A particular point to note is the authors' finding that Ericksonian therapy resulted in the same level of improvement as brief dynamic therapy, without the client needing to discuss the complaint.

There is no empirical evidence available on the role of Ericksonian therapy in the treatment of attachment disorders; however, there are many case examples in videos of Erickson's work and also writings about his work (Erickson, 1985; Erickson & Rossi, 1979, 1989; Haley, 1973; O'Hanlon, 1987; Rosen, 1992; Wake, 2008; Zeig, 1980, 1985).

Neurolinguistic psychotherapy

Neurolinguistic psychotherapy (NLPt) emerged from the early modelling of the linguistic patterns of Erickson, Satir, and Perls, by the co-founders of neurolinguistic programming (NLP), Bandler

and Grinder. In the mid 1980s, therapists in the UK became interested in NLP and its application in the therapy field. By 1996, a
formal therapy body for NLPt developed as an off-shoot to the
Association of NLP, and therapists McDermott and Jago (2001),
Lawley and Tomkins (2005), Gawler-Wright (1999, 2006), and Wake
(2008) began to integrate the application of NLP in therapeutic
work, such that it is now recognized as a brief psychotherapy.

Neurolinguistic psychotherapy is defined as:

- "a therapy of what is possible; it opens for the client and therapist a voyage which is genuinely into the unknown" (McDermott & Jago, 2001, p. 11).
- "a systemic imaginative method of psychotherapy with an
  integrative–cognitive approach. The principal idea of Neurolinguistic Psychotherapy (NLPt) is the goal-orientated work
  with a person paying particular regard to his/her representation systems, metaphors and relation matrices" (EANLPt,
  2008).
- "a specialised form of Neuro Linguistic Programming (NLP).
  The idea is that we work from and react to the world as we
  construct it from our experiences rather than directly from the
  'real world'. We build our own unique models or maps of the
  world. Although all such maps are genuine to each of us, no
  one map is fully able to represent the 'real world'. Further,
  NLP is a way of exploring how people think, identifying
  success and then applying these successful actions or even
  beliefs in ways that work" (NLPtCA, 2006).

Working principles of NLPt

NLPt is fundamentally a constructivist psychotherapy working
with the dynamic reality of the client's subjective experience.

Wake (2008) defines the underlying assumptions of NLPt as:

- the client is the expert on their problem and therefore the
  expert on the solution. (If they knew how to create the problem, they will equally know how to "un-create: the problem);
- the client's problem is how they structure their subjective
  experience and it is therefore possible to change their subjective view through "how" rather than "why" questions;

- the client has unlimited resources and flexibility of behaviour and it is a matter of facilitating the client to access and utilise these resources;
- the client will have their own internal map of the presenting "problem" and will have developed a series of behaviours in response to this map;
- these behaviours have been generalised over time;
- each of the behaviours that the client presents with will have a purpose and function;
- the purpose and function of each of the behaviours will have been positive for the client at some point in time;
- behaviour is precisely that it is not the identity of the person and the person is always more than their behaviour;
- behaviours are contextually dependent therefore there will be a time when they don't "do" the behaviour i.e. the solution already exists;
- the client will communicate their internal landscape or "map" in ways that are both conscious and unconscious;
- the purpose of therapy is to increase choice for a client and facilitate them to a more resourceful state than they currently have access to;
- that a small change in the structure of the client's reality can result in a major change in their subjective experience;
- the therapist can't not project their perception of the client onto the client;
- the main focus of therapy is towards outcomes (pp. 18–19).

Gawler-Wright (2005) and Wake (2008) both consider that NLPt is a relationally based psychotherapy. The role of the therapist is to develop a therapy whereby, through co-created relational activity, the client can apply their existing resources, attention, and strengths to develop new possibilities of neurolinguistic and sensory reality.

Evidence base for NLPt

There is limited evidence for the effectiveness of NLPt as a psycho-therapy for clinical conditions. Einspruch and Forman (1985) reviewed thirty-nine studies on NLP as a generic psychological intervention that had taken place between 1975 and 1984. Their study identifies a number of components that questioned the validity of the research that had been undertaken previously. They identify that although NLP is testable and verifiable, any previous research was methodologically inadequate. They conclude that it is not possible to determine the validity of either NLP concepts or whether NLP-based therapeutic procedures are effective for achieving therapeutic outcomes. They make recommendations that empirical investigations are conducted to test the validity of NLP as a model of psychotherapy.

Two pieces of research emerged from this original review by Einspruch and Forman, one by the researchers themselves, who, in 1988, were able to demonstrate marked improvement in a group of thirty-one phobic patients within a multi-faceted treatment programme using NLP and Ericksonian approaches. Measurement instruments used were "Mark's phobia questionnaire" and "fear inventory", and the "Beck depression inventory" pre and post treatment. The researchers conclude that NLP holds promise for becoming an important set of therapeutic techniques for treating phobias.

A further piece of research was conducted by Genser-Medlitsch and Schütz (1997). This study demonstrated, through a comprehensive evaluation of fifty-five patients, that neurolinguistic psychotherapy is an effective modality of therapy in accordance with its therapeutic objective. The clients all had severe *DSM* conditions, such as schizo-affective disorder, psychosis, psychosomatic tendencies, depression, or dependency problems, and most were also on medication. Patients in the control group all had milder symptoms. Measurements were conducted at three points in time of changes in individual complaints, clinical psychological symptoms, individual coping strategies, and locus of control tendencies, using the linear rating scale model (LRSM) and the linear partial credit model (LPCM). After therapy, the clients who had received NLP scored significantly higher (76%) in each of the measured areas and experienced a reduction in clinical symptoms. The researchers concluded that NLP is effective according to the therapeutic objective.

NLPt does demonstrate effectiveness of intervention in context-specific anxiety or phobia disorders. Koziey and McLeod (1987) consider the effectiveness of neurolinguistic psychotherapy with individuals who are experiencing anxiety following being raped.

Ferguson (1987), Krugman et al. (1985) and Hale (1986) reviewed the application of NLP in anxiety related to public speaking. The resolution of phobias is reviewed by Einspruch and Forman (1985), Kammer, Lanver, & Schwochow (1997), and Liberman (1984). Allen (1982) reviewed the effectiveness of NLP with individuals who have a phobia of snakes.

Provocative therapy

Provocative therapy was developed by a psychiatric social worker, Frank Farrelly, and is a brief therapy that uses the principle of reverse psychology. The model encourages clients to work with paradoxes by focusing on the more positive aspects of their situation by "lampooning" their self defeating and negative thoughts and behaviour. Therapists who use this approach claim that the effectiveness of the therapy is down to each individual therapist and their ability to empathize with the client and to create imaginative and spontaneous imagery, ideas, and responses to presenting issues. There is no "standardized" provocative therapy, with therapists each adopting their own unique approach to therapy.

Working principles of provocative therapy

Hollander, Dawes, and Duba (1990–2000) define thirty-nine different strategies of behaviour and thinking patterns that Farrelly used in his work with clients. These are grouped into seven different categories.

1. Ongoing behaviours, which are behaviours that the therapist does all or most of the time.
    (a) Make physical contact.
    (b) Use a joking tone of voice.
    (c) Non-verbal mirroring.
    (d) Use anecdotes.
    (e) Focus intently on the client.
    (f) Don't help the client.
    (g) Don't keep track of the session.
    (h) Be easily distracted and act very dumb.

    (i) Remember that you are provoking appropriate behaviours.

2.   Conditional behaviours that the therapist does if the client reacts in a certain way.
    (a) Go for the emotion.
    (b) Red–green colour blindness—if the client reacts with strong emotions and asks the therapist to stop, the therapist continues.
    (c) Describe the client's strong non-verbal reactions.
    (d) Ask for specification.
    (e) Trance work.
    (f) Responding seriously to traumatic experiences.
    (g) Reflect incongruence.

3.   General provocative tools.
    (a) Interrupt the client.
    (b) Mimic the client.
    (c) Illustrate the impact of the client's behaviour on others.
    (d) Misinterpret the client's confusion or other communication problems.
    (e) Lamely protest claims of progress.
    (f) Ineptly undermine favourable feedback.
    (g) Have them repeat strong conclusions.
    (h) Broadly and extensively dramatize your fantasies.

4.   Reacting to problem statements.
    (a) Do some more of that, think some more of that, feel some more of that.
    (b) Daliesque solutions.
    (c) Absurd explanations.
    (d) Overemphasize the client's assets to the total exclusion of the problem.

5.   Reacting to self concept.
    (a) Exaggerate perceived negative self concept.
    (b) Exaggerate negative body image.
    (c) Exaggerate cultural stereotypes.

6.   Therapists/consultants internal processes.
    (a) Get into the giggling state.
    (b) Be warm.
    (c) Listen to your own inner guides.
    (d) See internal television sets.

7.   Strategic patterns.
      (a)   Reverse the blame between client and life.
      (b)   Take sides.
      (c)   Demand that the client be interesting.
      (d)   Act crazier than the client.

Evidence base for provocative therapy

There is no researched evidence base for this therapy. The Association for Provocative Therapy provides a series of case studies of the work on their website (www.associationforprovocativetherapy. com).

Rational emotive behaviour therapy

Rational emotive behaviour therapy (REBT) was developed in 1955 by Ellis, emerging from his analytically-based work in marriage, family, and sexual therapy, with Ellis recognizing that the primary purpose of therapy is to ensure that people were "shown how they could live peacefully with themselves" (1962, p. 3).

Dryden (1996) defines REBT as a therapy that

> holds that humans are essentially hedonistic (Ellis, 1976); their major goals are to stay alive and to pursue happiness efficiently . . . that people differ enormously in terms of what will bring them happiness, so rational emotive behaviour therapists show clients not what will lead to their happiness but how they prevent themselves from pursuing it and how they can overcome these obstacles. [p. 306]

Working principles of REBT

REBT holds a number of theoretical assumptions that consider the image of the person and concepts of psychological disturbance and health, including the acquisition and perpetuation of psychological disturbance and the human change process (Dryden, 1996).

As a constructivist psychotherapy, REBT operates from the underlying principle that humans construct irrational beliefs, which result in distorted perceptions that then get acted out at an emotional level. Thought processes are divided into those that are considered rational, that is, they help the individual achieve their goals, and those that are irrational, that is, they prevent the individual achieving their goals. Irrational beliefs are considered to be rigid, illogical, and a distortion of reality.

Froggat (1997) identifies twelve principles that enable an effective life. These are:

- self knowledge;
- self acceptance and confidence;
- enlightened self interest;
- tolerance for frustration and discomfort;
- long range enjoyment;
- risk taking;
- moderation;
- self direction and commitment;
- flexibility;
- objective thinking;
- acceptance of reality.

There is a strong emphasis within REBT for the client taking responsibility for their own psychological wellbeing, and the primary aim of REBT as a therapeutic process is to enable clients to overcome their irrational beliefs and achieve goals that support the individual. Dryden (1996) considers that REBT can be effective in brief therapy if the following seven factors are present in the client:

- the person is able and willing to present her problems in a specific form and set goals that are concrete and achievable;
- the person's problems are of the type that can be dealt with in eleven sessions;
- the person is able and willing to target two problems that she wants to work on during therapy;
- the person has understood the ABCs (model of inferences, cognitions and emotions/behaviours) of REBT and has indicated that this way of conceptualizing and dealing with her problems makes sense and is potentially helpful to her;
- the person has understood the therapist's tasks and her own tasks in brief REBT, has indicated that REBT seems potentially useful to her and is willing to carry out her tasks;
- the person's level of functioning in her everyday life is sufficiently high to enable her to carry out her tasks both inside and outside therapy sessions;

- there is early evidence that a good working bond can be developed between the therapist and the person seeking help. [p. 314]

Evidence base for REBT

There is evidence of grounded research into the theory and efficacy of REBT. David and Avellino (2003) produced a synopsis of REBT research and identified that REBT is demonstrated as effective particularly where consequential measures are used to assess the impact on factors that are not directly related to the presenting problem, such as physiological measures, rather than direct relational components to the treatment, such as changing irrational beliefs. REBT is also equally effective in clinical and non-clinical populations and also in group or individual therapy. There is a correlation between the training of the therapist and the results of the therapeutic intervention, as there is in the ratio of therapeutic hours to outcome: that is, the more hours of therapy a client has, the more positive the outcome for the client.

Self relations therapy

Self relations therapy was developed by Gilligan and has its philosophical roots based in Ericksonian therapy. Modelling Erickson, Gilligan (1997) developed an approach to psychotherapy that focuses on the sense of self and four states of consciousness: happiness, health, helpfulness to others, and healing of self and others. Self relations views these changes in states of consciousness, both positive and negative, as providing opportunities for personal growth and development, with each individual moving through cycles of death and rebirth as new identities and opportunities are formed.

Working principles of self relations therapy

Similar to the view of Erickson, Gilligan views symptoms as an awakening within the personality rather than symptoms of neurosis. Self relations therapy (SRT) views this disturbance as an experiencing of a major shift in clients' identity and "crisis", representing both opportunity and danger, that, if managed appropriately, can result in major growth for the individual where the energies are channelled well, or danger if the energies are not channelled towards the growth of the individual.

There are six major premises to SRT (Gilligan, 2004).

- *Each person has a centre.* This is a primary intelligence rather than an intellect, an invisible presence that is a somatic knowing and experiencing.
- *The river of life flows through the centre.* All experiences are held in the body and are expressed through the body. SRT enables the client to literally flow through their body their own experiences rather than freeze in a flight/fright/fight response.
- *The river brings both happiness and suffering.* There is recognition within SRT that life will bring both positive and negative experiences, and that many people remain watchful to protect themselves from experiencing the negative. SRT proposes a third way of being, based on centring, extending life energy, and maintaining a relational connection, enabling the client to be open to suffering without being overwhelmed by it.
- *To navigate the river, a second (cognitive) self develops.* This cognitive self has a relationship to the somatic self, and it is through resonance between these two selves that a greater relational self can emerge.
- When the two selves harmonize, a third (relational) self emerges. This is an intelligence that exists within the relational field. SRT enables the client to learn to trust and connect with the relational field. It is by staying connected to their centre and the relational field that the client can respond to the challenges that life can bring.
- *So many roads, find a path with a heart.* SRT focuses on the uniqueness of each person and focuses on the importance of noticing, supporting, and accepting all aspects of the person. SRT enables the client to see the problem as their solution.

SRT focuses on the notion of the triunal mind. The somatic mind, the cognitive mind, and the relational field mind. Each mind has basic level functions and generative level functions.

- *Somatic mind.* The basic level of this mind is the survival instincts. The generative level of this mind is to be able to hold and contextualize emotional experiences. This occurs through a process of centring, where the client is able to manage experiences outside of their normal identity, for example, high levels of stress, trauma etc.
- *Cognitive mind.* The basic level consists of the rules that enable us to manage our social and psychological world. This basic level will experience difficulties in thinking outside of the box. The generative level of this mind allows for creative thinking, systemic identity, and resonant intentionality. It is through this process of meta-cognition that sponsorship occurs, where the self can use every experience to awaken to the goodness in the self and the world and develops a relationship between the two. It is through this process that the positive aspects of symptoms and problems can be harnessed. It is here that both/ and concepts are held.
- *Field or relational mind.* At a basic level, these are the constraints of boundaries that hold us in our existing identity or patterns of behaviour. The generative level enables transcendence beyond boundaries and moves the client beyond the problem to the space beyond. It is here that expanded awareness occurs.

Evidence base for self relations therapy

There is currently no empirical evidence base for SRT. Videos of casework are available at www.stephangilligan.com

Solution focused brief therapy

Solution focused brief therapy (SFBT) emerged out of the work of the Palo Alto group of therapists in the 1970s who were questioning the more traditional and scientific approaches to mental illness (Watzlawick, Weakland, & Fisch, 1974), and the solution orientated hypnosis work of Erickson and Rossi (1979), and Haley (1973). As this work continued, the therapists recognized that every problem will also always contain its solution. Therapists Berg and Dolan (2001), Berg and Kelly (2000), Berg and Reuss (1997), DeJong and

Berg (2001), de Shazer (1991, 1994), and Miller and de Shazer (2000) continued to develop this notion with a model of solution focused brief therapy emerging. A variation of SFBT has been developed by O'Hanlon (2000, 2003), referenced as possibility and inclusive therapy.

Working principles of solution focused brief therapy

SFBT has at its core a number of assumptions.

- Respect for the client's wishes for a more desirable state of being.
- The client has the ability to shape their lives.
- Therapy is brief and focuses on solutions rather than problems.
- Problems do not happen all of the time; therefore, by finding these times, the client will be doing positive things that they are not aware of.
- By bringing these small successes into awareness, and repeating them, clients become more confident and positive about their lives and their future.
- By becoming more hopeful and focusing on the future, people begin to feel more empowered as their preferred future is realized.
- Because the solution is already inherent within the client, it is easier to repeat than to learn new behaviours from someone else, enabling the therapy to be brief.
- As a person has more successes, they become eager to make more changes.

    Three basic questions underpin SFBT (BRIEF, London).

- What are your best hopes from this therapy?
- What would your day-to-day life look like if these hopes were realised?
- What are you already doing and have done in the past that might contribute to these hopes being realized today?

    The task of the therapist is to trust that the client has the answers to these questions and to ask the questions in such a way that the client can answer them. Beyond these three basic questions, the process of therapy consists of the following.

- *Negotiating the contract*: rather than the therapist asking "How can I help you?", the responsibility for the solution stays with the client, for example, "What are your best hopes from this meeting?" Where the client offers a negative motivation for change, for example, "To stop hating myself for drinking so much", the therapist asks, "So, if you were to imagine that this begins to happen, if you stopped drinking so much, what do you think will happen then?"
- *A preferred future*: this process involves the client defining an agreed goal, and then developing a detailed description of its realization, focusing on the client's preferred future, rather than the present and past unwanted behaviour. Clients are shown to have more success in achievement of the goal if the detail of its achievement is concrete, mundane, stated through actions, and sufficiently small in chunk size so that no aspect of them is beyond a client's current ability.
- *What are you already doing*: this involves identifying with the client what is already working and using hidden resources to move towards the preferred future. SFBT assumes a principle that the more problems a client has experienced and survived the more hidden resources they are likely to have.
- *Solution focused conversations and scaling*: clients often present for therapy expecting the therapist to need to know and understand the detail of the problem. The assumption is made by the therapist that it is more helpful to know what to do next rather than know why a previous event went wrong. By working with the exceptions to the problem state, it is possible to use these times of exception as possible ways forward. By using scaling, where 10 represents the outcome and 0 the opposite, the client's position on the scale will allow for questioning of what resources they have used to be at that point rather than lower. It also enables the client and therapist to focus on what they have done in the past when they have been higher up the scale.
- *What's better*: when the client returns for subsequent sessions, the therapist will usually begin with the question, "What's

better?" This will bring to the session the improvements that the client has made, what difference this has made to others areas of their life, and also how the client will know that the improvement continues.

Evidence base for solution focused brief therapy

There is a substantial evidence base for SFBT, with at least three meta-analyses conducted reviewing the outcome research for the approach.

Gingerich and Eisengart (2000) conducted a meta-analysis of the outcome research for solution focused brief therapy. Fifteen studies were included in the review, of which five studies were considered to be well controlled. Four of these studies found SFBT to be significantly better than no treatment or standard institutional services, and one study compared SFBT with interpersonal psychotherapy and found SFBT produced equivalent outcomes.

Stams, Dekovic, Buist, and de Vries (2006) and Kim (2008) conducted further meta-analyses of 21–22 studies and evidenced small effects in favour of SFBT for personal behaviour change, suggesting equivalence to other therapies. Within these studies, Knekt and Lindfors' (2004) and Knekt et al.'s (2008) randomized control trial compared SFBT with short term psychodynamic psychotherapy, demonstrated no significant difference between the therapies, but showed that SFBT was faster. However, at three-year follow-up, gains were maintained with the long-term psychotherapy only.

Subsequent to these meta-analyses, Forrester, Copello, Waissbein, and Pokhrel (2008) conducted an evaluation of an intensive family preservation service for families affected by parental substance misuse and demonstrated less time spent in care after 3.5 years follow-up for the intervention group. This study has relevance for clients with attachment-related problems.

Summary

Many of the therapies summarized here provide an evidence base for working with attachment problems or disorders that could stem from early attachment relationships. Few of them provide the gold standard for evidence—the randomized control trial. Yet, as demonstrated in the following chapter, there is an increasing body of evidence that supports the effectiveness of some of these therapies. Additionally, as each of these therapies are viewed in the light of what is now emerging through neuroscience and the developing brain, I would propose that further research can be conducted that will illuminate some of the factors that Norcross (2002) considers as essential to therapy.

The inner world of the client through the brief therapies

Introduction

This chapter integrates the current understanding within the brief therapies of core belief structures, sense of self, and internal processes, and links these to the theories of object relations and the later development of attachment disorder.

One of the challenges that the brief therapies face is the ability to demonstrate effectiveness of therapy in relation to outcomes, and, where brief therapies have evolved from the more traditional approaches, to gain recognition, respect, and credibility with the longer-term psychodynamic and analytic approaches.

In reviewing some of the underpinning theories of psychodynamic and analytic approaches, my intention is to present alternative and briefer therapeutic interventions to specifically respond to attachment-based problems.

Most brief therapies aim to affect the subjective relationship that a client has to their current reality. In considering the underlying principle of object relations theory that later informed the development of attachment theory, it is clear that Klein (1928) worked to alter the subjectivity of relationship to the internal object, viewing the client as a "subjective agent within a subjective world of relationship, conflict and change" (Gomez, 1997, p. 34). This resonance with the subjectivity of relationship, which is an inherent component of many of the brief therapies, is also found in the work of other, later object relations and attachment therapists, such as Winnicott, Fairbairn, and Bowlby.

Object relations theory is an accepted approach to working therapeutically with clients, yet, this theory remains fraught with the same tensions as other therapeutic approaches. Research into the theory is beginning to demonstrate a scientific evidence base for therapeutic outcomes and there is sufficient practice-based evidence and case analysis to suggest that there is an epistemological base to using this theoretical approach, particularly when it is linked to the later developments of attachment theory. It is now possible to measure changes in attachment scores as a result of psychotherapeutic intervention, with comparable scores for psychodynamic and CBT approaches (McBride, Atkinson, Quilty, & Bagby 2006). In a Cochrane review, Abbass, Hancock, Henderson, and Kisely (2006) identified that short-term psychodynamic therapies demonstrated moderate therapeutic gains for specific clients.

This chapter includes a qualitative study of the relationship between object relations theory and one of the brief therapies, NLPt, and is presented as a discussion point to encourage a greater reflection of the psychodynamic process as it occurs in brief therapy.

The inner world of the client in the brief therapies

The subjective world of the client is present to a lesser or greater degree in each of the brief therapies referenced in Chapter One. Summarized in Table 1 are the brief therapies, the theoretical principles of the subjective processes and inner world, and the evidence base in working with attachment-related problems.

Subjectivity of relationships within psychodynamic literature

In reviewing the theories above, it is clear that beliefs within most of the brief therapies consider the sense of self in relation to others

Table 1. Evidence base for attachment work.

Therapy	Theoretical principles of inner subjective world	Evidence base of working with attachment-related problems
Cognitive analytic therapy (CAT)	Chronic and self-limiting patterns of emotional expression and behaviour. Beliefs were once effective (maladaptive) solutions to experiences and emotions in childhood that have now become strategies that are used as coping mechanisms.	Mace, Beeken, and Embleton's (2006) comparison of post treatment outcomes of inexperienced psychiatrist trainees conducting either brief psychodynamic therapy or brief integrative psychotherapy resulted in eight of the nine trainees achieving more favourable results with the psychodynamic intervention. There are a number of ongoing studies utilizing CAT with clients with varying degrees of borderline personality disorder, including those with relationship difficulties (The SPeDi Trial, www.shef.ac.uk/spedi/; Kellet, Bennett, & Ryle, 2009).
Cognitive–behavioural therapy (CBT)	Early learning experiences and trauma can lead to idiosyncratic beliefs. These cognitive distortions include arbitrary inferences, selective abstraction, over-generalization, magnification and/or minimization, personalization, absolutist dichotomous thinking (Beck, Rush, Shaw, & Emery, 1979).	McBride, Atkinson, Quilty, and Bagby (2006), in a RCT, studied fifty-six patients with adult attachment insecurity and compared inter-personal psychotherapy (IPT) and CBT. Outcome measurements included Beck Depression Inventory, Six-Item Hamilton Rating Scale for Depression, and the

(*continued*)

Table 1.   (*continued*)

Therapy	Theoretical principles of inner subjective world	Evidence base of working with attachment-related problems
	Maladaptive schemata arise from family experiences and become the primary mode for responding to situations (Young, 1990). "Interpersonal processes have a reciprocal relationship with intrapersonal processes. Social context forms part of cognitive formulation. (Mansell, in House & Loewenthal, 2008, p. 26). "Negative *automatic* thoughts occur fleetingly . until brought into awareness; counterproductive avoidance strategies push distressing material outside awareness; cognitive formulation incorporates life experience including trauma" (Mansell, in House & Loewenthal, 2008, p. 20).	Rating Scale Questionnaire to assess adult attachment. The results demonstrated that patients with higher attachment avoidance experienced a greater reduction in depression severity with CBT compared to IPT. Siqueland, Rynn, and Diamond (2005) conducted an RCT of CBT and a modified combination of CBT and attachment-based family therapy for anxious adolescents. Methodology used was the Beck Anxiety Inventory, the Hamilton Anxiety Rating Scale, the Beck Depression Inventory, and the Hamilton Depression Inventory. The study suggests that both methods of therapy are effective.
Eye movement desensitization and reprocessing (EMDR)	Negative self beliefs are verbalizations of emotions that are present and will often have developed as a result of traumatic incidents (Shapiro, 2004).	Van der Kolk (2005) has demonstrated the effectiveness of EMDR in attachment-based trauma. Shapiro (2002) and Madrid, Skolek, and Shapiro (2006) demonstrated that EMDR can be an appropriate treatment for bonding difficulties. Soberman, Greenwald, and Rule

(*continued*)

Table 1. (*continued*)

Therapy	Theoretical principles of inner subjective world	Evidence base of working with attachment-related problems
		(2002) were able to demonstrate that EMDR was effective in reducing memory-related distress and problem behaviours in boys with conduct problems.
Ericksonian therapy	Beliefs and behaviours are context dependent, and that the unconscious represses painful memories of infantile experiences. Erickson believed that by changing the context of a problem or belief, this would change the behaviour that resulted from the belief (Erickson & Rossi, 1989).	No empirical evidence available on the use within attachment disorder.
Neurolinguistic psychotherapy (NLPt)	Core beliefs are drivers that influence subjective reality and may be rooted in a sense of hopelessness, helplessness, or worthlessness (Dilts, 1990). Watzlawick (1978) proposed that core beliefs are primary to the individual, who holds them true and unalterable.	Crandell (1989) presents a case history demonstrating the effects of brief therapy for adult children of alcoholics and the impact that this can have on developing self-care behaviours. De Miranda and colleagues (1999), in a Cochrane-based review, used an RCT to study the impact of the application of NLP to mothers of children enrolled in a day care centre of a shanty town. Measurements used were children's development (Bayley scales), home environment variation

(*continued*)

Table 1. (*continued*)

Therapy	Theoretical principles of inner subjective world	Evidence base of working with attachment-related problems
		(HOME), and maternal mental health (SRQ). Pre and post comparisons were made in terms of the child's psychomotor development, the home environment, and maternal mental health. The study demonstrated that there were positive effects on the home environment from the intervention.
Provocative therapy	Beliefs are part of the demonstration of the client's ambivalence towards life's goals and relationships (Farrelly & Brandsma, 1974).	No empirical evidence available.
Rational emotive behavioural therapy (REBT)	Irrational beliefs (demands, awfulizing, low frustration tolerance, and self or other downing) lead to dysfunctional emotions and inferences, and rational beliefs (preferences, anti-awfulizing, high frustration tolerance, and self/other acceptance) lead to functional emotions and inferences. Demand beliefs is the primary core irrational belief (Ellis, 1962).	Gonzalez et al. (2004) conducted a meta-analysis of the effect of the use of REBT on children and adolescents, and demonstrated that it had the most effect on disruptive behaviours and in younger children. Validity of this analysis cannot be assessed.
Self relations therapy	Beliefs are held in the cognitive self, which is the medium between the self and the world. Within symptoms, the sense of	No empirical evidence available.

(*continued*)

Table 1.   (*continued*)

Therapy	Theoretical principles of inner subjective world	Evidence base of working with attachment-related problems
	self disappears, contracts, dissociates, or becomes nullified. The challenge for the cognitive self is the principle of relatedness (Gilligan, 1997).	
Solution focused brief therapy (SFBT)	SFBT is a postmodern, social constructionist approach that sees the way language is used in social situations as constructive of how one views the world. The model does not have theoretical principles of the client's inner subjective world. Irrespective of the severity or perceived intractability of the belief, there are times when the client does not "do" the problem. By focusing on this, the client finds solutions that already exist within their resources.	Gingerich & Eisengart (2000) conducted a review of fifteen controlled studies that demonstrated preliminary support for SFBT as an effective modality. Five studies were considered well controlled. Clinical conditions ranged from depression, opposition disorder, parent–child conflict, prison, recidivism, adolescent offending, marital relationships, addiction problems. Nardone and Watzlawick (2004), in their book on solution-orientated research and treatment of eating disorders, demonstrated effective protocols for the treatment of eating disorders. It is to be noted that Nardone and Watzlawick are not SF therapists, and use solution-orientated approaches in their work. Nardone and Portelli (2005), and Nardone and

(*continued*)

Table 1. (*continued*)

Therapy	Theoretical principles of inner subjective world	Evidence base of working with attachment-related problems
		Watzlawick (2002) published ten years of research that demonstrated treatment in 3482 cases involving a large range of pathologies, such as panic, phobia, eating disorders, and obsessive compulsive disorders, resulting in an 88% success rate. These studies have not been reviewed as a meta-analysis.

with varying degrees of emphasis on the impact that the subjective awareness of self can have on psychological health. The psychodynamic literature, object relations theory, and the later development of attachment theory propose concepts regarding the relation of the Self to the Other.

Gomez (1997, p. 1) defines object relations theory as "used in the philosophical sense of the distinction between the subject and object. Our need for others is the need of an experiencing 'I' for another experiencing 'I' to make contact with".

Bowlby is seen as a developer of object relations theory, and his work in this area spawned a separate school of psychotherapy, attachment theory (1969). Attachment theory holds similar principles to, and is built on, object relations theory. It focuses on the primacy of the need for a relationship and the relational structure of the self.

Each of the therapies discussed in Chapter One have their own theoretical approach, and yet, in reviewing the theories of Klein, Bowlby, and other attachment therapists, Winnicott and Fairbairn, there is evidence of considerable parallels to these briefer forms of therapy. To develop greater understanding of this area and to begin to determine if there are parallels within the experience of brief outcome orientated therapists, I have conducted a qualitative study to consider if there is a relationship between the subjectivity of the core belief processes of NLPt and object relations theory.

The relationship of brief outcome-orientated neurolinguistic psychotherapy (NLPt) and object relations theory

A grounded theory study (Glaser & Strauss, 1967) was conducted of the core belief processes of neurolinguistic psychotherapy and links were then made to object relations theory. Neurolinguistic psychotherapy is a relatively new modality of psychotherapy and is predominantly brief in intervention. Object relations theory, as a depth and long-term psychotherapy, emerged out of psychoanalytic theory. It provides a conceptual framework that places the self in relation to other, that is, the object, at the centre of the therapy process. By including this study within this book, I hope that other brief therapists will develop some of the findings and create credible sources of evidence for the efficacy of brief therapy.

The study considers the therapist's perception of beliefs as they are presented by clients in therapy and compares the therapist's experience with conceptual principles that are present in object relations theory.

Through a process of convenience and theoretical sampling, semi-structured interviews were conducted with six therapists who are trained in neurolinguistic psychotherapy. Analysis of the data was conducted using a thematic analysis of conceptual maps. The study aimed to identify whether relationships exist between the two different theoretical approaches, the inherent meaning of the therapy process, and how therapists perceive that clients represent beliefs in therapy.

Methodology

Six therapists were selected, using a combination of convenience and theoretical sampling. Of the therapists selected, four operated from a pure NLPt theoretical basis, and, of the remaining two therapists, one was also trained in family therapy, integrative and psychoanalytic theory, and one was also trained in Ericksonian therapy.

Semi-structured interviews were used for this study to develop a grounded theory understanding of the concepts and themes that exist for therapists regarding clients' representation of their belief structures. Questions used for the semi-structured interviews were:

1. How do you identify a client's core belief structures?
2. What patterns, if any, have you observed in the core belief structures in a number of clients?
3. What theories, if any, have you developed about how these core belief structures have arisen within the client?
4. In working with a client's history story, what observations have you made about the generalization of belief structures?

The second set of interviews was guided by the emerging data, which were beginning to demonstrate that the role of the therapist was a key component within the therapy. The same initial question was asked; however, the researcher focused subsequent questions on the role of the therapist during the client session.

Subsequent to each interview, the data was transcribed and analysed to consider emerging themes (Table 2). The main themes that had emerged as possible theories in the first set of interviews included:

*   role of resistance in therapy;
*   therapy relationship;
*   three patterns of behavioural response that clients gave;
*   what the therapist is doing in the session;
*   relationship of self to the world;
*   recognizing and working with patterns.

The emerging themes were discussed with two colleagues to enable the researcher to test out understanding and to challenge thinking. Credibility and confirmability was enhanced by ensuring that there was sufficient evidence within the transcripts to support the themes. There were sufficient data emerging from the study subjects to ensure that disconfirming data were excluded from the

Table 2. Emerging themes.

	Meaning unit (total number of times concept mentioned)	Therapist total (total number of therapists referring to the concept: $n=6$)
Main Category 1 The therapist's approach to working with beliefs		
(a) How beliefs are identified		
● Identification processes	33	5
● Working with patterns	29	5
● Incongruence in the client	14	3
● Psychiatric labels	6	3
(b) Holding and seeking possibilities		
● Creating possibilities	38	6
● Working towards outcomes	16	4
(c) The therapist's role		
● Therapist identification of their role	23	4
Main Category 2 The client's process		
(a) Psychodynamic processes		
● Resistance	112	6
● Transference and countertransference	46	6
● Conflict	10	4
(b) Unconscious processes		
● The structure of beliefs	27	6
● Repression of emotions	11	5
● Non-cognitive thinking	10	2

(*continued*)

Table 2.   (*continued*)

	Meaning unit (total number of times concept mentioned)	Therapist total (total number of therapists referring to the concept: $n=6$)
• Fundamentalism	9	4
• Fabrication	8	2
(c) The client's sense of self		
• Negation of self	24	4
• Valuing self	12	5
(d) The client's belief structures		
• Where beliefs come from	56	6
• Flexibility in thought and emotion	19	5
Main Category 3		
Relationships		
(a) The therapy relationship		
• Providing agency for the client	43	5
• Respecting the client's world	23	5
• The therapist's reactions	21	6
• Connecting	15	4
• Trusting	14	3
• Holding	6	2
(b) The client's perspective		
• Relationship of self to others	27	6
• Client's attributing their condition to others	9	2
Main Category 4		
Professional practice		
(a) Safety for the client		
• The client being safe	14	4
• Scope of practice	12	4

(*continued*)

Table 2. (*continued*)

	Meaning unit (total number of times concept mentioned)	Therapist total (total number of therapists referring to the concept: $n=6$)
● Ceasing therapy	9	3
(b) The professional role		
● Being supervised	12	3
● Ongoing development of the therapist	3	3

study. Only data that were present in four or more of the study subjects are included in these findings. Data are only included where the study subjects give a clear description of their experience, which can be demonstrated through examples. The study is limited in that only six subjects were interviewed, where ideally 8–20 subjects are used.

A member check was conducted at the University of Surrey NLP Research Conference in July 2008. Six NLP therapists from across the UK and Europe were present during this oral and PowerPoint presentation. The initial findings from the data were presented and a verbal response given to the researcher. Comments included a need for links to object relations theory where this can be made, and a call for further extensive research into this area. Within the time constraints of the study and limited number of study subjects, it was not possible to check out the validity of the data through triangulation. The author attempted to address this through the checking of coding categories by another researcher, which resulted in a change to some of the categories. Because of the lack of research into this area, it was not possible to conduct a comparative study with other studies. There is comparison within the findings between the data sets from the study subjects.

Results and interpretation

Four main categories emerged from the data:

- the therapist's approach to working with beliefs;
- the client's process;
- relationships;
- professional practice.

The therapist's approach to working with beliefs

Dilts (2000) describes beliefs in NLP as

> one of the key components of our "deep structure". They shape and create the "surface structure" of our thoughts and actions in many ways. Beliefs determine how events are given meaning, and are at the core of motivation and culture. [p. 97]

The theoretical concept of working with a client's belief structures is core to NLP, and, therefore, it would be expected for therapists to refer to this as a key area of focus in their work.

In considering beliefs within object relations theory, Bowlby proposes that internal constructs about the self are formed from early attachments and clients develop internal working models of themselves and others. These working models are made up of expectations, beliefs, emotional states, and judgements and rules that determine either the processing or exclusion of information (Bretherton, 1987). Blatt, Levy, and Shaver (1988) suggest that by integrating psychoanalytic theory and cognitive developments, proposed by Piaget, it is possible to understand the affective components of self representations and that these will be "global, diffuse, fragmentary, and inflexible to increasingly differentiated, flexible and hierarchically organized" (p. 407).

Winnicott (1960) holds a similar view, in that individuals will develop a "false self" as a way of coping with inner conflict states.

Fairbairn (1943) considers that beliefs are a way of the patient representing loyalty to their internal objects. He proposes that clients hold on to these familiar constructs to prevent the world disintegrating into the experiences of early trauma, and that the role of the therapist is to provide security and trust before the client can consider abandoning their internal objects.

Within object relations theory, there is a relationship between social cognition, the individual's sense of self, and significant other representations that make up the individual's core beliefs about themselves. The Social Cognition and Object Relations Scale (SCORS) (Hilsenroth, Stein, & Pinsker, 2007; Westen,1995), is a recognized and validated rating scale for object relations theory that is used as a way of measuring beliefs about self in relation to others. The scale consists of eight variables. The variables include:

1. Complexity of representations, which measures how accurately a client perceives internal states in themselves and others, including how they manage their relational boundaries, and their ability to integrate the positive and negative aspects of their personality.
2. Affective quality of relationships, which measures the individual's expectations of others in the relationship, including how they describe previous relationships.
3. Emotional investment in relationships, which assesses the client's ability for emotional intimacy and emotional sharing.
4. Emotional investment in moral standards, which assesses the client's ability to relate to others through moral concepts and levels of compassion.
5. Understanding of social causality, which measures the capacity for understanding human behaviour.
6. Experience and management of aggressive impulses, which assesses the client's ability to manage aggression appropriately.
7. Self esteem, which assesses self concept.
8. Identity and coherence of self, which assesses levels of client fragmentation and integration.

How beliefs are identified

All therapists were clear that they are working with beliefs and are able to identify the processes that they use. Therapists consistently referred to the client's lack of conscious awareness of their beliefs (unattributed quotes throughout the following sections), and that the beliefs are usually of such a high order and at identity level that the client may not always be aware of how limiting the belief structure is, whereas the really deep core beliefs, they are hidden so deep, that often they don't have awareness of them.

This is supported by Bowlby's theory that beliefs are partly conscious and partly unconscious, and usually not completely consistent or coherent (Blatt, Levy, & Shaver, 1998). Bowlby (1973) proposes that the rationale for keeping beliefs outside of conscious awareness is to defend the person from a threat to the self. There is consistency with NLPt theories that consider repression of beliefs as being defensive and self-protective functions (Wake, 2008).

Therapists describe a number of ways to enable the client to recognize their existing behaviours and find different ways to reframe these.

> The analogy is to allow the client to recognise what ingredient they put in . . . the client to recognise how it has been cooked and to recognise that they no longer have to take the bowl of soup, or taste the same spoonful of soup consistently . . . that allows them to see things not only from the way that they have always seen them, but allowing them to see them in a fuller context, rather than just their individual experience.

Gill and Hoffman (1982) refer to enduring beliefs resulting from what the client expects in relationships, and that ambiguity created by the misconstruing of other's behaviour leads to problems and distress for the client. It is by interrupting these generalizations in belief structures that the client can develop a more effective capacity for forming good relationships.

Irrespective of the process by which the therapist reframes the client's experience, the therapist always leaves the responsibility for change with the client.

> I talk about taking responsibility and taking action and all of that stuff. So that is, if you like, the frame around . . . I talk about that is where I am coming from . . . and . . . if they go "um, I don't want to talk about that", you say, ah, hang on a second. We talked about, all that time back, do you remember when, and they go "Oh yeah", that. *Right*, can we just ex . . . can we just talk about that bit of resistance, that's not like you. You know, we have talked about all of these other things over here and there is this one thing over here.

In some instances, the therapist would ensure that the work with the client was paced so that they could take responsibility for their own change:

> what we would do then is identify an element of this that he could deal with or an element that he'd dealt with prior to this that we could bring, you know, use as a resource in this sort of process.

Therapists refer to their need to be where the client is, in many different ways, which reflects McDermott and Jago's (2001) notion of pacing the client.

> I won't try and argue anybody out of the belief because they need to have that belief for whatever reason.

Another therapist refers to this as

> it tends to now just evolve and emerge through, as the relationship develops. I am seeking to avoid *me* saying "ooh, I think this, that or the other", is true in this, that or the other context.

Within the literature on object relations, and working within the attachment relationship, it is likely that this approach of ensuring that the client takes responsibility for change can only be effective with those clients who have relatively secure attachment processes. Mallinckrodt, Wei, Larson, and Zakalik (2005) suggest that clients with secure attachment have positive working models of self and others and will be able to access their own internal sources of affirmation, whereas clients with high attachment anxiety have negative internal working models and, therefore, a limited ability to draw on internal resources for reassurance, hence, they will need to look externally for this. The NLPt model does not allow for suggestions or reassurance on the way forward; rather, it assumes that the client has all the resources he or she needs to achieve results. However, it does consider opportunities for validation through one of its presuppositions of respecting the client's model of the world (Dilts, 2000, pp. 1001–02).

Therapists were respecting of the behaviours and beliefs of clients, and will pace the current belief structure, making it all right for the client to experience what they are experiencing in therapy, allowing the client to do all sorts of things, to do happiness, to do sadness, to do anger, to do fear, to do rejection, and for me to be the rock.

And

Client's got to be allowed to do what client wants to do.

These processes link with positive reassurance that clients may be seeking. The therapist who referred to being "the rock" epitomizes the role of the therapist in providing reassurance for those with attachment anxiety, and, by allowing clients to initially seek reassurance from the therapist, the client can be encouraged in self reinforcement so that they build up a positive self esteem, which is demonstrated to reduce depressive symptoms (Fuchs & Rehm, 1977).

Five of the six therapists worked with patterns represented by the client, with one therapist referring to a structured model,

those are ones that obviously I've done work on are, are in the Pond model, and . . . permission, possibility, obligation, necessity and desires.

Other therapists referred to a more metaphorical description of how they identified patterns within their client's representations:

I describe it as, the pattern of inverse house of card building,

which the therapist goes on to describe in more detail,

so that when you build a house of cards, each card stands on the next, when you do a core belief, instead of a house being with the base at the bottom and small at the top, it's stood on one card, which is the core belief. An inverted house of cards.

Another therapist gives a similar description:

One of my analogies is that a diamond has many different facets, and if I look at one facet and when I turn it and look at it from a different light, and that seems to be something that, what I would consider to be core beliefs is that they do reoccur at different times.

Bowlby (1969, 1980) describes this pattern of behavioural and belief representations as a series of mental representations of the self, others, and self interactions, and that this combination leads to the acquisition of dependent traits, which includes attitudes, beliefs, and behaviours.

Within this section, it is clear that therapists working within the modality of NLPt identify, analyse, and reframe patterns of belief structures, which adheres to variable 8 of the SCORS measurement tool. Therapists are able to identify a coherence of self with clients that clearly assesses levels of fragmentation and integration.

The holding and seeking of possibilities

Klein's work, although controversial at times, did demonstrate her love and respect for the children that she worked with. Within her analysis of children, she would often provide comfort, hope, and play as a way of enabling a more positive future for the child. There is evidence of this in the SCORS scale, which includes an assessment of self esteem as a way of evaluating self concept.

Universal across all therapists is the notion of creating possibilities for the client in the here and now. This is done in two distinct ways. Therapists are able to work with the current range of behaviours and create different choices from this:

> just putting them in a different order, then having a different choice.

and,

> I can say "instead of having problem X, what would you rather have?" and that leads us down another avenue.

This focuses the client towards an outcome state rather than a problem state. Within this process, the therapists consider that the generation of other possibilities is something that they share with their clients:

> what I say to people is, I can, I can create *choice*, in the work we do together, what you do with that *choice* is *your* affair.

The second way of working with possibilities is for the therapist to hold in their own construct the notion of the opposite of the presenting problem.

> I will hold in my head "well yes they could very well be depressed, but they may not be depressed".

And

> I can ask about when problem X doesn't occur, and that leads us down another avenue.

This includes working with possibilities to redirect the attention of the client to another possibility or meaning of the current pattern of behaviour:

> generate another possibility and to get them to work totally with the physiology and absolutely exaggerate the physiology, and just at least have three so it's not a dichotomy, it's a triangulation of possibilities . . .

and, more specifically,

> I was often offering C a *menu* of *possibility* in terms of what those interpretations might be like on the one hand.

Although possibility and outcome-based approaches do not necessarily fit within the field of object relations theory, recent research into compartmentalization, or schizoid processes, has demonstrated that the more clients work with positive compartments of their psyche the greater is the association with positive feelings about the self and the greater is integrative organization, whereas, if negative compartments are accessed, this contributes to negative mood and low self esteem. By offering a more integrated structure, even when the negative is accessed, the client is more likely to minimize the impact of important negatives (Showers & Kevlyn, 1999). This view supports Wake's (2008) theory that working with the neuroscientific components of affective states towards a future orientation can facilitate rapid change within a client.

The role of the therapist in working with beliefs

The therapy relationship and psychodynamic process is discussed within another category; however, there is a strong recognition of the significance of the therapist's role within the interviews. Although the therapists do not refer directly to the notion of attachment theory, except in one instance, it is clear that the role of the therapist as object is a significant concept for all therapists.

> My role is to provide them with the *rock* around which they can do what they need to do . . . that of almost being like a rock and the tide came in and the tide came out.

Another therapist refers to this in a very insightful way:

> Because the real, the real *work* there is just in the relating . . . I can think of a couple of people where I have worked with maybe 30–50 hours over a *long* time, and you know, and one was pretty awful. . . . Really nasty, systematic abuse, prolonged abuse, that this person had been subjected to over many years as a young person. So the first thing, above all else is about building trust and just *relating* week on, every other week, whatever it was. And *creating* a *platform* or a scenario in which, actually it is OK, to start to *just* let that little inner self start to show. So that's what I was saying when I talk about defensiveness or protecting, it is a massive generalization.

The attachment relationship is not discussed within NLPt theory, and for most NLPt therapists is considered to be insignificant. Wake (2008) and Gawler-Wright (2005) both contest this view, and recognize that the role of the therapist in assisting repair of early attachment relationships is crucial. Each of the therapists within this study also considered that they had a significant role within the therapy process.

Winnicott (1960), Fairbairn (1952), and Bowlby (1969, 1973, 1980) all considered that, within therapy, the relationship with the therapist provides a heuristic clue to early attachment relationships. Both Wake and Gawler-Wright provide a description of Dujovne's (1990) summary of the role of the therapist in object relations therapy. She refers to

> the experience of the "good" therapist challenging the predominantly negative bond with the "bad" object and puts the patient in

touch with its "goodness". Thus, the experience of the nurturing therapist–parent seems to dislocate the patient's internal dissociation by bringing ambivalence into the foreground. The dislocation occurs because the "good/bad" split fails, the internal reality of sadness cannot be denied and omnipotence turns to vulnerability. [p. 477]

This is represented in the narrative of the two therapists above, who both consistently refer to being there for the client, and allowing the client to do whatever the client needs to do in the moment.

The client's process

The primary processes that are at play in the client's world within object relations theory are the processes of splitting, introjection, projection, and the schizoid and depressive positions (Gomez, 1997). Emotions such as envy, rage, anxiety, fear, annihilation, depression, guilt, anger, grief, and sadness are all considered to be resultant of the early life experiences of the client. Each of these emotions will get played out in the therapeutic relationship.

The NLPt therapists were fully aware of the client's process within therapy, and although the language used was dissimilar to that used within object relations theory, the semantic meaning of the experiences bore strong relationships to some of the concepts found within object relations theory. These are summarized below, with examples given.

Psychodynamic processes

Within the literature of NLP, there is little to support the notion that it is a therapy that involves the therapeutic relationship. Wake (2008), the EANLPt website, and Gawler-Wright (2006) all hold an alternative view and propose that the therapy relationship is key to enabling a client to find solutions and new behavioural choices.

It is only when the therapist develops a truly responsive relationship of trust and understanding with clients that the unconscious can become conscious, what is held non-verbally and somatically, can be sponsored and validated. [Wake, 2008, p. 174]

Three main categories emerge that reflect the psychodynamic nature of therapy. All therapists refer extensively to working with resistance, with each of them highlighting awareness and utilization of the transference and countertransference process. Four of the therapists also referred to working with conflict in the sessions.

Resistance

Each therapist used different terms to describe the kinds of resistance that they encounter during therapy. They refer to clients "being stuck", "rigidity", "fundamentalism", and "having tantrums" as a wide range of ways that they experienced with clients as they accessed the core belief structures.

> we go down a particular route in our information gathering and it hits a stuck place . . . we go round it another way, and it gets back to that same stuck place and back to the same stuck place . . . There's the belief, and the first bit for me is what I call the dead end . . . if you're *stuck* there rigidly you're going to have difficulty.

Therapists expressed their many attempts to move the client beyond this point.

> the steps that I had taken in the therapy, and the options of therapy available didn't create the pace of change that I would expect in therapy . . . no matter what happens, that doesn't shift.

One therapist considered that the stuckness was driven by a fear within the client.

> 'there's a great deal of fear of changing the interactions that they have and that creates stuckness in the client, but they don't know how to change.

Therapists also proposed that the stuckness was caused by neurological deficits.

> It's as if there is no awareness of the possibility of doing it differently. And there is nothing in the neurology that offers, there's nothing to compare it with the catalogue in the mind that they're OK with what shall I try in its place.

Resistance in the psychodynamic world was first coined by Freud, who noted that clients would often be unwilling or unable to voice their thoughts and feelings because the superego was repressing the conscious or unconscious less acceptable impulses. Within psychodynamic and analytic therapies, resistance is used as part of the therapy process, and within NLPt there is no theoretical concept for recognizing, managing, and working with the psychodynamic model of resistance, yet all six therapists reported resistance as being an inherent part of the therapy sessions. NLPt views resistance as a sign of lack of rapport, and would propose that therapists increase their level of rapport to counter resistance. The literature would suggest that when the therapist is meeting unconscious resistance and is unable to respond to it through normal therapeutic processes, such as rapport, this links the client back into the "consistent non-responsiveness of parents in childhood" (Fraley, Davis, & Shaver, 1998). This process results in the individual protecting himself further by avoiding connection in the therapy relationship.

Transference and countertransference

Most of the therapists had a working knowledge of transference and countertransference at a theoretical level, and each therapist also clearly articulated their awareness of how the transference was acted out in the therapy relationship. This strongly contrasts with the blocks that the therapists were experiencing when they met with resistance.

> I fall into a role as a father figure to a particular client, that is the archetypal role that I play, you come to your dad for an answer.

There was also a strong recognition of when the therapist was being affected by their own countertransferential response,

> I felt that I was getting further into his negative state, so I wanted to do something other than that.

Therapists were able to refer to examples of when the therapy relationship had been significantly affected by the transferential process, with therapists referring emotionally to the impact that the client had on them.

Two examples are given of this, the first where the client acted out in a concerning way his own reactions to the therapy,

> The world's a frightening place, I haven't got the capabilities to do all this, YOU do and you also have the responsibility to look after me, so if I'm feeling the world's a frightening place, that's because you've not done your job by me, so I now have justified anger against the people in my life and against you as a professional, because it's your job to do it. But, the world's a frightening place, so I'm going to stay frightened, I'm not going to do anything about it because I can't, I'm incompetent, so . . . er . . . and I'm not here to work on "how I become competent to deal with it", because I believe it's your job to make the world a better place for me. [Client's response]

Bowlby (1960) refers to this as the patient acting like the "detached" child. His approach to therapy proposes that the role of the therapist is to support the client as they go back and work through the repressed emotions of sadness, hopelessness, and wishes for love that were missed out on in the phases of despair and protest. Klein also refers to this, and suggests that the role of therapy is to help clients work through the depressive position in the attachment relationship between therapist and client.

The second example provides insight into the negative and positive countertransferential responses that the same therapist experienced:

> I was quite flattered by the referral, I thought, "Ooh, the person, I held this person in quite high regard, the person who referred the client had recommended me, and with hindsight, the feeling of flattery, was something [laughs] to really pay attention to.

and in his negative countertransference, he refers to,

> the person came in and went all round the office picking up, was really invasive with my space, making comments on things.

This process of working with transference is supported by Bond, Hansell, and Shevrin's (1987) view that locating evidence of transference in psychotherapy is essential. Five steps are identified by these authors in identifying location judgements of where a client's transferential problem exists (pp. 736–749). These steps consist of:

1. Identifying the "object" when multiple persons are referred to rather than a single individual.
2. Determining what to do when an account of a relationship with one person is interlaced with recollections about others as well.
3. Distinguishing between a "specific interaction" and a "general account of a relationship".
4. Rating the "completeness" of a relationship episode.
5. Identifying where a relationship episode begins and ends.

All therapists were limited in their approach to working with the transference, and it is clear, within the syllabus of training in NLPt, that transferential processes are not taught as mainstream.

Conflict

The primary conflict that arises in object relations theory is that of conflict between the good and bad object. Fairbairn provides an effective description of this (see Table 1).

There is recognition among the therapists that many clients experience levels of unconscious conflict where they are caught in a paradoxical or double bind situation.

> people are in conflict because they've got conflicting beliefs that are in two different modes of operation.

Therapists consider that it is the attempt by the client to resolve his or her conflict that often causes even greater conflict. This paradoxical process is highlighted in two examples,

> What they are doing is seeking confirmation that they have no value, although they assume they are seeking confirmation of value

and,

> there was a lot of guilt associated with not having her at home and guilty about not going every day, and also desire to protect her own boundaries and having some space for her.

This matches Fairbairn's notion of the "anti-wanting I", or the internal saboteur, which results in the client rejecting his own neediness and, therefore, not getting what he wants.

One therapist proposes a theory of how this process is set up within a client:

> If the child comes up with a counter example and the parent will dogmatically say, "no you are wrong", then that can set up conflicting ideas with in the child-"I thought I was right but I've been told I was wrong".

Unconscious processes

This category demonstrates five principle processes through which the client's belief structures can be understood within their unconscious processing. The structure of the client's beliefs is outlined, as is the client's ability to manage raw emotions through repression.

The structure of the client's beliefs

One of the questions asked within the semi-structured interview concerned the structure of beliefs. Within NLP, there is very little information on the structure of core beliefs, with Dilts (1990) referring to three core processes of Being, "helplessness", "hopelessness", and "worthlessness".

Only one therapist referred specifically to the work of Dilts in considering core belief structures:

> If it has to do with making myself feel *better*, then I feel in terms of NLP terms what we're looking at is the sort of stuff that Dilts has talked about of helplessness, hopelessness, worthlessness.

Another therapist did not refer to Dilts specifically; however, they did refer to the notions included within Dilts's model:

> they're usually around whether people have worth or not, whether they deserve or not and whether they exist or not, whether there's space for them in the world or not.

Other therapists used another model:

... are in the Pond model, and so ... erm ... permission, possibility, obligation, necessity and desires ... quite a few people will have ... erm ... a belief in an attachment around "unless this, not this", "unless this happens, I can't have that", "unless I'm this, I can't be that", "unless they give me this, I can't do that".

Another therapist used a metaphor to explain her understanding of belief structures.

a bowl of soup, everything is put in and heated up, and then when you dip the spoon in, you will get an element of all the ingredients, but you won't necessarily get a piece of carrot, a piece of potato in that one spoonful.

It is clear from this study that NLP therapists do not have a fixed construct of belief structures as proposed by Dilts. Klein's theory proposes that splitting is unique to each person, and that the infant uses splitting to ensure that each of the components are separated into manageable components. Klein holds the view that splitting has two main domains, "good" and "bad" objects, and these are then further differentiated into the initial relationship with the mother, and, in later life, with other people, objects, and processes. Klein goes on to say that this manifests as destructive anger within the depressive position, the paranoid–schizoid fear of annihilation, and the fear of loss of the identity, resulting in worthlessness. These relate directly to Dilts's theory of "hopelessness", which is manifested within the depressive position, "helplessness" within the paranoid–schizoid fear position, and "worthlessness" within the fear of loss of identity where the infant feels wholly bad and worthless.

Fairbairn holds a similar view to Klein, proposing that in the schizoid position, where love is destructive, the client experiences intense meaninglessness, and in the depressive position anger and hate result in despair, which again matches Dilts's theory.

Winnicott relates anxiety states to the three processes of "holding", "handling" and "object-relating". His theory suggests that where "holding" has not been handled well, the baby experiences a threat to his Being, matching Dilts's theory on "hopelessness". In "handling", where this is not managed well by the mother, the baby experiences having no relation to his body, feeling unreal or depersonalized, and he ends up with no reference point, similar to Dilts's view of "helplessness". Winnicott's third process is that of "object-relating", where the infant develops a fascination with, and desire for, the external object, which commences with feeding and relationship to the nipple. In anxiety states influenced by "object-relating", the infant experiences a sense of separateness from others, resulting in futility and loneliness. This is less clear in relating to Dilts, in that it appears to affect all components of Dilts's "beingness".

Bowlby relates to anxiety states through attachment processes. He considers that securely attached children are more likely to form effective relationships with others. The insecure–ambivalent child will have an internal self structure that is unlovable, based on an unpredictable other, which mirrors Klein's paranoid–schizoid position. The insecure–avoidant child has an internal self structure that is not worthy of care, which results in repression of anger, which mirrors Klein's depressive position.

The repression of emotion

What was clear among all therapists was the amount of energy or emotion that is present within the belief structures as the therapist begins to work with them. This matches the early description of meeting with resistance.

> A pushing away, a getting nearer, and I think often when you get near to the core of things, the tenderness of things, unconsciously at least, people do push away, you do get push back, which can be a clue that "ooh, I'm on the right track here".

Therapists voice the accessing of these unprocessed emotions in a number of different ways:

> I'm aware of there's a plateau, well there probably is a plateau, that is then followed by accessing a very powerful emotion which is being repressed or feared previously.

There is also a concern that the client may not have the resources to deal with this level of emotion:

so no, not with everybody, so to drop her into a completely emotional space, I think would drop her down a black hole, she wouldn't have any structure or any, if anything to deal with that.

Fairbairn considers that this mechanism is set up to ensure that we reject the intolerable aspects of our self. The client continues to project inwards their own "badness" and can therefore continue to see the external person as good enough. Fairbairn (1943) describes this as "moral defence", whereby an outward sense of security is retained at the expense of internalized insecurity and conflict.

Winnicott (1960) provides a different perspective on this, which supports the therapist's comments above. When holding and protection is not present, the infant feels an overwhelming sense of annihilation, which the adult then masks by covering up with a false self, and an external appearance of coping. Winnicott suggests that if these states are accessed without the appropriate support structures, this can result in psychosis.

The client's sense of self

Each therapist had a perception that clients have difficulty holding a positive sense of themselves, and that the role of therapy is to enhance or develop a stronger sense of self for the client. Most of the therapists referred to a negation of the self:

They are actually starting and seeking proof that they have no value;

and

it was so core to whether she existed or not;

and

Is it OK for the person to claim space for themselves or, my basic way of understanding it, whether they hold a space in the world or not;

she was *completely* within her reason to feel *utterly* negated and that this meant she had no worth as a person, she has no value, that is what they are saying.

This is then contrasted with the development of self value:

> The value is something that externally you may recognize in certain situations, in that situation your value was met, and you were valued;

> Because I think it is important for the client to value themselves . . . and to value themselves enough . . . that they can form an opinion, that the opinion is right and they can influence others.

These statements support the notions presented by Klein, Winnicott, and Bowlby. Although the NLP therapists do not refer to the development of the self through object relating, it is clear that they are working in accordance with an internalized view of the self, and that this is based on either "good" or "bad" introjects.

Klein's (1960) theory on the development of the self is determined by the merging of internal and external realities. The individual sense of self is always influenced by both components and is driven by an unavoidable internal conflict. Klein holds the view that, although we grow through stages of development, we will inevitably return to the perspective of the paranoid–schizoid or depressive positions at points of anxiety and conflict in our lives.

The client's belief structures

Evident within the interviews was the view that clients had an idea of how they had developed their own beliefs and this was supported by the therapist's recognition and identification of patterns.

Flexibility in thought and emotion

Therapists were able to consider what was present when a client was not resistant, hence providing a contrast frame for considering the process of resistance.

Causes or indicators of this flexibility in the client were voiced as,

> You can resolve the fear around falling off the bicycle and be OK about it, so there's an adult understanding of the processing in what is going on and you can go through several stages of that, and

resolve lots and lots of things . . . When they've had experience of working, of shifting between thought and emotions to resolve an issue and they've learnt that they can do that process with safety anchors within the room, then it's OK for them to start to bring those into the room, of bringing depressed, disidentified emotional states . . . skill in the client that they've learnt that they can resolve stuff for themselves, though they may have done it with me coaching in the room, and they may often have experiences outside the room when they have done change work themselves without needing my presence and so what they have realized is, that they can keep themselves safe and do change work.

What the therapist is demonstrating here are variables 1, 2, and 5 of the SCORS scale. The client is demonstrating an understanding of their own internal states in relation to others, the affective quality of their relationships, and also the social causality for understanding their own and others' behaviour. Although the therapist does not use the theoretical framework of attachment theory, he is demonstrating a clear positive attachment process, whereby the client is responding to the responsiveness of the therapist as a positive and responsive attachment figure (Bowlby, 1973).

Relationships

Relationships are consistently referred to in the interviews and these are categorized into two concepts; the therapy relationship, and, the client's perception of relationships. It is the relationship of the self to others that is a core component of object relations theory, and is the basis of the SCORS measurement scale.

The therapy relationship

Providing agency for the client

One therapist sums up each of the other therapists with his description, and of the agency role that the therapist provides.

I can see the client now sitting there, and . . . I am holding my hands, probably shoulder width apart . . . my palms are open, as if I imagine holding a giant beach ball. It's how I see this thing. Or a big kind of globe, or some spherical thing like that, anyway.

And the client, is holding, if the client is bringing that into the room, they have never seen it before. And they don't know what this thing is, and neither do I. But they bring it in, they get it out, we kind of, you know, turn it round and we look at it, we rotate it. "You know, what is this, what is this thing? And what is it here for and what does it do?" All that stuff, so it is this process of exploration and when they leave, between each session, I hand it back to them, they take it with them, and when they come back again, we will get the thing out again, and so it goes on. And I think by setting it out in that way, it demystifies, it takes me off any kind of pedestal, which I am very keen on, staying off any kind of pedestal. And it makes me accessible, it makes the therapy accessible, it makes it a normal, natural occurring thing between two, it's back to Jung's thing, between two people. And I think that is hugely helpful. And I think it relaxes people and it just takes the, a lot of the angst, a lot of the heat out of what is, you know. As you say, you drive out here, all of that, you are going to see a therapist, oh my god, what is wrong with me, all that sort of stuff that might be going on for someone. And they sit down, and nnnnnn, and a bit tense maybe, and [it] just goes, you can just see the whole thing just melting away.

It is recognized within attachment relationships in object relations theory that there is a need among anxious individuals to seek validation and reassurance from others. The therapist here is demonstrating his own ability to provide validation, reassurance, and Winnicott's (1963) "holding" and "object-relating", with the therapist providing attunement to the client's needs and inner state.

Respecting the client's world

The flexibility of behaviour among therapists in respecting each client's world is also apparent, with therapists either adopting means by which they can work solely with each client as a unique being,

I have almost like a little ritual there though, in terms of working with an individual, is that I do something prior to stepping in this room with a client just to prepare myself . . . so that is why I have

> little rituals that clear the space inside my head so I can come to this new,

or, they adapt their style as they respond to each client.

> With some clients I have to go very cognitive, so the lady with, the daughter, where the mother was abusing the daughter, a bullying Mum in effect, that was very, very cognitive, very different process using the board and pulled her completely out of that space of emotion,

whereas the same therapist uses a different approach with another client,

> so a long-term client where we sort of walked up to, we had explored some of the really deep felt emotions around things and allowed those emotions to come up . . . Anchors we had built previously about self acceptance and about . . . erm . . . him coming to terms with, for him, why he'd done what he'd done and presuppositions and him doing the best that you could at the time, and doing whatever it was that he was able to do.

The principle process in object relations therapy is to use the therapy relationship to work with the paradoxical emotions that are held within the client. Dujovne (1990) suggests that the therapist's role is to acknowledge the emotional states within the client and use these to assist the client to acknowledge and integrate the split-off aspects of the self. The therapists in this study demonstrate their ability to provide a "good enough" therapist–parent role to assist connection in the client and a way of assisting the client to develop faith in relationships.

The client's perspective

One main theme emerged in this category: the sense of the client's self in relationship to others. One therapist summarizes the thoughts of others by referring to a process of reconciliation:

> The second thing is to bring at a level *reconciliation*, reconciliation between the belief and between themselves for example, reconcili-

ation between themselves and other members of the family, wider circle, work colleagues, religion, higher order society.

This is expanded on by another therapist, who considers that it is resolving this relationship of self to others that is the key to successful therapy:

> what is it about me that makes people *react* the way they have done to me? . . . er . . . and what is it about *others* that makes them react the way they have to me?

It is clear that the therapists are working with clients to develop a more integrated sense of self and are influencing variables 1 and 2 of the SCORS scale. The therapists in the study highlight their ability to work within NLPt processes to develop a capacity within the client for self-reinforcement and reconciliation of the "good" and "bad" aspects of the self.

Within the notions discussed above, and as therapists work to understand, reflect, and change clients' belief structures, there is a strong emphasis for the client on how they perceive others in their world and how this affects their relationships.

> it served him, that's the problem, because he's so good at making people listen to his complaints and it's "Oh my god I'm sorry, I'm sorry I didn't . . . oh, oh" and he just dries [sucks in] them up and then moves on to the next.

This is carried across a number of different examples,

> I'll get reflections of the client in terms of how they think they might be seen by third parties . . . one of his beliefs is that he is always expected to take care of other people and its not OK to have time for himself . . . because then the attention that they seek from others is limited by what they expect to receive in return.

Therapists were able to move clients on in their relationship with others by becoming the "other" in therapy, reflecting object relations theory that the therapist becomes the object in therapy.

> And if they believe that they can be right as well as wrong, and if they believe that they can influence others . . . then when they go

out into the *big bad world* and meet people, then if someone disagrees with them, then it doesn't destroy them and it doesn't send them back into a negative loop . . . it becomes more give and take and they become a much more robust, healthy, normal, happy, functioning person.

Gomez (1997) comments that most therapeutic approaches can work with the object relations perspective, particularly in relation to assessing a client and his needs, or where difficult or conflicting processes occur in therapy.

Professional practice

Some of the categories that emerged included the need to ensure that safety was maintained for the client and that therapists worked within their scope of practice, including the use of the supervisory relationship. There is little within object relations literature regarding professional practice. The schools of object relations theory require that therapists are in ongoing psychotherapy during their training and also remain in supervision. As ongoing personal therapy during training is not a core requirement for NLPt therapists, I have included components of professional practice within the findings, as they do relate to, particularly, the countertransferential process.

Safety for the client

Each therapist clearly worked within their scope of practice and demonstrated their desire to keep the client safe. Therapists varied in their approach to how they managed this, with some using risk assessments:

I think what I actually did was go into risk assessment of whether she was entertaining what this meant for her;

and others focusing on the relationship:

with a role just round making sure that this place was safe for him so we could begin to explore the sort of processes that were going on.

Although therapists are clear about their scope of practice, there is a level of unconscious incompetence earlier in the findings regarding the role and place of resistance, transference, and countertransference. One of the therapists in the study clearly referred clients on when they were outside of their theoretical framework. Other therapists were keen to ensure that safety was maintained for the client, although they did not have clear ideas of what the therapeutic programme of care would be for clients where resistance was actively being demonstrated in therapy.

Therapists continued to highlight this as they discussed their professional role. Some therapists contained this by staying within the therapy that they had received training in:

> it was inappropriate for me to continue to work with them, because I was not offering what they needed long term to achieve the outcome. That is that the therapy I have been trained in and I have knowledge of isn't a broad enough therapy to encompass that need, and there are therapists and therapies that may well be able to encompass their needs. My background training doesn't have that total extensiveness to allow me to encompass it.

Other therapists referred to their inexperience:

> I think for me it was about my inexperience, as a practitioner that . . . erm . . . maybe I hadn't been as fully present as I wanted to, maybe notice what was happening as I was asking questions.

Conclusions and recommendations

This study demonstrated that there is a relationship between the core belief structures of NLP and object relations theory. Many of the processes and patterns present within object relations theory are found among the therapy processes of the NLPt therapists. It is of significance that all therapists work with an internal representation of the self, and that this is described as having positive and negative attributes. Therapists are aware of the role of transference and countertransference in therapy, and are also attuned to resistance, although there is a lack of theoretical understanding and application back into practice the process of working with resistance.

The main conclusions of the study can be separated into:

- the attachment relationship and resistance;
- affective states and outcome orientation;
- belief structures;
- splitting processes.

The attachment relationship and resistance

The attachment relationship is core within the work of these thera-pists. The traditional NLP model of therapy would focus only on outcome, which is likely to be highly effective for clients with posi-tive attachment histories. Where clients have experienced negative attachment relationships, the process of outcome-orientated non-psychodynamic therapy that is provided by NLPt and other brief therapies is unlikely to address early attachment needs. In model-ling the work of Satir, Perls, and Erickson, Bandler and Grinder focused predominantly on the linguistic structure of the therapy process. Satir (1972) was a family therapist and, as such, worked with the relationship constructs within the family and often found herself, as part of the attunement process, adopting particular roles within the family. Perls (Perls, Hefferline, & Goodman, 1973), as the founder of Gestalt therapy, worked with the projections of clients, often becoming the mirror for the "bad", split-off aspects of the psyche. Erickson also used positive attachment relationships within his work, particularly in his relational therapy, described by Haley (1973).

It is recommended that the current teaching of NLPt based ther-apy includes the attachment relationship. Dilts (2000) has included this in the consideration of the imprinting processes of Lorenz (1970), and this could become the basis of a wider understanding of the development of the self from an NLPt perspective.

The emergence of resistance as a theme in the therapy is very apparent. Therapists are clearly working with this, and, as such, this is likely to bring to the fore both transferential and counter-transferential responses. It is, therefore, essential that NLPt includes at its core training a greater level of personal exploration and thera-peutic change for students wishing to become therapists. This can be supported in a way that respects the outcome and individualistic

nature of the modality, while at the same time ensuring that therapists are emotionally and psychically equipped to respond appropriately to resistance states.

Affective states and outcome orientation

NLPt is an outcome-orientated psychotherapy and each of the therapists demonstrates the outcome focus that he or she utilizes when
working with clients. There is a strong emphasis in NLPt on the
linguistic and programming aspects of the modality. There is
limited emphasis on the neurological components and, where this
does exist, it is limited to references to operant conditioning and
Pavlovian responses. Wake (2008) has extensively researched up to
date theories and developments in neuroscience and has brought
these into the modality. Within the therapists' interviews, each of
them demonstrated an ability to recognize and work with affective
states. By adding the recent work by Schore (2003a,b), Gerhardt
(2004), and Pert (1997), NLPt can bring neuroscience and theories
on affective states into an outcome-orientated frame, thereby
affording effective therapeutic change through brief interventions.

Belief structures

The purpose of this study was to identify whether there is a relationship between the core belief structures of Dilts and those
conceptualized within object relations theory. Evidential within the
material are the concepts as they are described by Dilts, although in
a different linguistic form. Certainly, by taking a meta perspective
on the material as it was reviewed, and by considering the entirety
of the therapist responses, observations, and theorems, it is clear
that parallels can be made between the two theories. The parallels
are summarized in Table 3.

Splitting processes

Fairbairn's model for splitting processes (Figure 1) is evident in the
work of the therapists. Within this process, as it is defined by
Fairbairn, there are some parallel processes that are occurring
within NLPt. There is a core sense of identity within individuals

Table 3. Parallels with attachment theorists.

Klein	Fairbairn	Bowlby	Winnicott	Dilts
Paranoid–schizoid position	*Schizoid position*	*Insecure ambivalent*	*Handling*	*Helplessness Worthlessness*
Fear of annihilation Fear of loss of identity Worthlessness	Love is destructive Meaninglessness	Not lovable Unpredictable other	No relation to the body Feeling unreal Depersonalized *Object relating* Separateness from others Futility Loneliness	
Depressive position Destructive anger	*Depressive position* Anger and hate Despair	*Insecure avoidant* Not worthy of care An other who does not care Repressed anger and longing	*Holding* Threat to being *Object relating* Separateness from others Futility Loneliness	*Hopelessness*

that relates directly to the central ego, and the libidinal connection to the object exists. As we grow and develop, we form ideal projections, that is, how we want to be perceived by others. This is clear in some of the descriptions of the therapists' work, where they are aware of clients who present an idealized projection of themselves and the resistance that they meet when this idealized projection is challenged. Within Fairbairn's model (see Chapter Three), splitting occurs between the libidinal and anti-libidinal egos and the rejecting and exciting objects. It is suggested from this study that the splitting, as it is demonstrated within NLPt, occurs between the sense of self with self, resulting in helplessness and worthlessness, and the sense of self in relation to others, resulting in hopelessness.

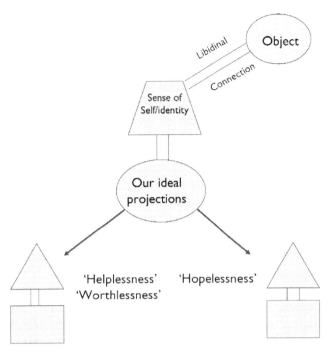

Figure 1.   Sense of self in relation to others.

Limitations of the study

The study is limited in design and can only be considered as a case study analysis. There were difficulties within the study that included the limited number of study subjects, and also the possibility that two of the therapists were being influenced by their wider training in other psychotherapies. Additionally, the experience of three therapists meant that they had pursued ongoing post-qualification training and reading into other psychotherapy approaches. These factors affect the reflexivity of the data, as does the lack of triangulation against other studies.

Further research

Further studies need to be conducted into the process of NLPt as a psychotherapy. This study could be used as a starting point for a comprehensive study with up to twenty participants.

work of Erickson, who appeared to be working with the attachment relationship, and whose work has informed Ericksonian therapists Gilligan (1997), O'Hanlon and Weiner-Davis (2003), and Gawler-Wright (2006), all of whom work in a co-created way to develop a more secure sense of self.

Object relations theory

Klein, as the founder of object relations theory, studied Freud in her early life and supported Freud's view that from birth the ego developed through its orientation to an external reality. However, she disagreed with Freud's view that there is a non-differentiated self at birth, and placed significantly more emphasis on the ego. Her theory can be summarized as one whereby all physiological instincts are driven by an urge to connect with an external object and, depending on the impulse being positively or negatively felt, will result in a drive to connect with the object either as a desire for, or to destroy, the object. Klein (1946, 1952, 1960) considered that these early impulses in relation to an object influenced our ongoing life, resulting in a continuous series of conflicts between the urge to love and the urge to destroy the object.

Klein's theory on the development of the infant included a number of stages. The paranoid–schizoid position refers to the first three months of life, where the baby is focused on managing the chaos of early life by splitting his relationship to objects within the world into good and bad parts. The baby takes in, or introjects, objects that he perceives as good parts and uses these to form his sense of self, whereas the baby does his best to defend against the objects that he perceives as bad parts, and will project these on to the other, which, when introjected back into the baby, results in further splitting and fragmentation.

By the second half of the first year of life, the baby moves into the depressive position. The baby experiences the world from a more real stance and, because of the earlier projection processes that have occurred, the baby begins to have mixed feelings about his carers. As the baby comes to terms with the different components of people around him, both the good and bad elements within them, he starts to experience different emotions, such as sadness, grief, guilt, and anger. As he begins to recognize that the good and the bad exist in his prime carers, he experiences a sense of loss, both of all that is good, because it is tainted with the bad, and of his own full sense of goodness. Klein suggests that as the child continues to develop, he works hard to repair relationships and please his carers, which assists him to gain a greater sense of emotional achievement. Klein attempts to analyse what this means for the child, and this then becomes the basis of Kleinian therapy.

Attachment theory

Bowlby presented his first paper on the importance of the role of the mother in understanding institutionalized or hospitalized children to the World Health Organization in 1951. He proposed that children who are deprived of the potential for attachment to a permanent mother figure would develop social, emotional, and psychological problems later in life. Bowlby held the view that the infant's attachment response is a survival instinct, and that this occurs at a critical point in the child's development, similar to the imprint process observed in birds (Lorenz, 1935). As he developed his theory, three forms of attachment disorganization were proposed.

Avoidant attachment

The child protects the parent from his own feelings for fear of upsetting or antagonizing the parent further. The child develops as a dysregulated organism, on the surface level appearing to be calm and placid, while underneath experiencing autonomic arousal with resulting increased heart and stress response as they work hard to suppress their feelings. If the child experiences this for prolonged periods, he will develop a reduced sense of self and an underlying anxiety response that results from the continuous suppression of his feelings.

Ambivalent, or resistant, attachment

The child experiences an inconsistent response from his parents. He will, therefore, keep his emotions close to the surface, so that as the parent begins to give him attention, he can make a bid for it to ensure that his emotional needs are met. This constant heightened state of awareness of the other's reaction or lack of reaction to the child will lead the child to over-exaggerate his feelings. The child will develop with a reduced sense of self and, as an adult, will often go headlong into emotional situations without being fully aware of the appropriateness of these.

Disorganized attachment

The child is brought up in a family where the entire organism of the family system is dysfunctional. This often results from parents who are experiencing trauma, for example, bereavement, or trauma within the relationship. The parents are unable to provide the basic structures of protecting the child for survival, resulting in the child growing up with no defence postures to protect himself. He is unable to manage his own feelings under pressure, resulting in inconsistent and sometimes unpredictable responses in adulthood.

*   *   *

Bowlby considered that the maternal object was the primary focus of libidinal energy and, like Freud, preferred to view this as occurring predominantly in the Oedipal period, bringing in the role of the mother in developing the internal world. In attachment theory, the primary attachment is to the mother or care-giver, with anxieties being a response to separation from the mother. By six months of age, the baby becomes aware of others, and secondary attachments are formed. It is at this age that "stranger" anxiety emerges, with the baby seeing the stranger as representing danger. Bowlby considers that it is quality of relationship, rather than quantity of time, that enables a secure sense of self.

In separation from the primary care-giver, the infant will experience three different stages.

Stage one results in protest. The child becomes distressed and will do everything to get her parent back. When the separation ends, the child responds with anger, relief, and anxiety, causing her to cling to her parent.

Stage two results in despair. If separation continues for too long, the child loses hope that the parent will return and becomes apathetic and withdrawn.

Stage three is apparent recovery, or detachment. The infant becomes interested in his surroundings, represses his relationship with the lost figure, and develops an attachment to the new carer.

Where a child experiences prolonged separation, this results in difficulties in relating to others, and may develop attachments to other objects, such as food or money.

Two other therapists, Fairbairn and Winnicott, also developed their own theories for the attachment relationship, building on Klein's work.

Ronald Fairbairn

Like Klein, Fairbairn studied Freud and also came to the view that the ego, or "I", began at birth as a dynamic structure (1952), with the primary aim of object-seeking. Fairbairn proposed that our strongest urge is for contact with others, and that we are driven by separation anxiety. Fairbairn differed from Klein, in that he viewed the more aggressive components of a personality as being a representation of blocked energy when contact with the primary object is denied. Fairbairn considered that individuals are born whole and that it is the failure in a relationship that causes splitting, or the schizoid position. These split-off aspects of the personality are then repressed inside the individual and held within the baby's subjective experience of external relationships. As the splitting process continues, the baby develops internal objects that are held as polarities of the good and bad components. These are viewed by Fairbairn as the libidinal ego, where the baby yearns for what he cannot have, which then becomes the exciting object, and the anti-libidinal ego, where the baby rejects the part of him that is attached to the rejecting object (for example, the part of him that is needy), then becomes the internal saboteur who despises the neediness (Figure 2).

Fairbairn supported Klein's view that the schizoid and depressive positions become the source of conflict and fear throughout life, and that individuals have a tendency towards one more than the other, with the schizoid position resulting in a sense of meaningless in life and the depressive position resulting in hating the person who is needed.

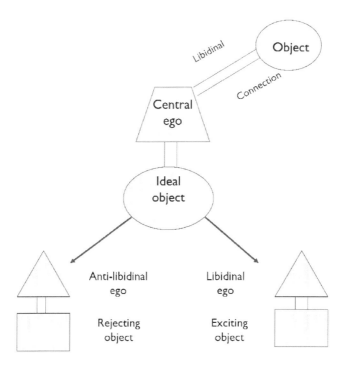

Figure 2. Fairbairn's organization of object relations.

Donald Winnicott

Winnicott's early experience in psychotherapy provided a balance between Freudian and Kleinian psychoanalysis. Winnicott provided a different perspective to Klein, in that he was more interested in what the theory meant in practice. He disagreed with Klein on the notion of instinctual conflict, and considered that we are born healthy and that a baby develops a sense of self through a "good enough" mother. His theory holds the view that the baby is preoccupied with the mother as the primary object, and that it is the mother's ability to contain the sense of oneness with the baby that provides a security within the infant's self. For Winnicott, life then becomes a process of moving through phases of illusion to disillusion, seeking a core sense of togetherness (1971).

Winnicott did not support the schizoid and depressive stances of Klein and Fairbairn, and, similar to Bowlby, he placed greater emphasis on the attachment relationship with the mother. He considered that the mother provides three main protection elements for the developing baby: holding, handling, and object-presenting.

Holding provides physical and emotional containment, resulting in a sense of coherence within the identity of the individual. Where holding has not occurred, the baby experiences having to hold himself, resulting in development of a false self that hides and protects the real self.

In handling, the role of the mother is to provide a sensitive and responsive touch. Where this has been a positive experience, the person will experience connection between mental, emotional, and physical capacities. Where this has not been handled well, the person develops a distancing from his physical needs and may have no relationship to his body.

Object-presenting is the way that the mother provides a perspective on the outside world to the baby. This begins with feeding, and where the mother handles this well, the baby develops a primitive sense of omnipotence and dual unity, whereby he develops a oneness and trust in the world. Where this is not handled well, the baby may fear being engulfed or taken over by others. This results in confusion over personal boundaries and a false sense of self, or, in severe cases, a separateness and isolation from the rest of the world.

Winnicott also included a theory of transitional phenomena, where the transitional object, such as a teddy bear, rag, or blanket is used to enable a transition between absolute and relative dependency on the mother. It also provides a connection to a sense of oneness in an individual who has a limited sense of omnipotence as they separate from the mother figure.

Modern theories on the developing brain

A combination of the theories presented by neuroscientists, psychologists, and psychotherapists (Damasio, 1994; Hart, 2008; LeDoux, 1998, 2002; Panksepp, 1998; Pert, 1997; Schore, 1994, 2003a,b) and the scientific investigative tools that enable structural understanding of the brain, such as magneto encephalography (MEG), magnetic resonance imaging (MRI), functional magnetic resonance imaging (fMRI), and positron emission tomography (PET) scans have enabled a greater understanding of the developing brain and the relationship of neural pathways to thinking and emotional processes.

MacLean's (1970) description of the triune brain (Table 4) is a useful starting point from which to understand the theories presented by others.

There are some excellent summaries of MacLean's work (Gerhardt, 2004; Hart, 2008; Schore, 2003a), and, rather than repeat these descriptions, I have included the main functions of each area of the brain that are particularly relevant when considering the attachment relationship.

Table 4. MacLean's triune brain.

Brain	System	Structures	Functions
Reptilian and diencephalon	Sensory	Brain stem and mid brain, consisting of: thalamus basal ganglia hypothalamus	Instinct Regulation of basic body systems Motor system Primitive emotional reflexes, e.g., flight, fright, fight response Towards and away from responses
Palaeomammalian brain	Feeling	Limbic system consisting of: Amygdala Hippocampus	Social emotions Mental and non-reflexive activity Memory Learned emotional responses
Neomammalian brain	Thinking	Neocortex Cingulate gyrus Parietal lobes Prefrontal cortex Orbitofrontal cortex Dorsolateral pre-frontal cortex	Mental and cognitive reasoning Making sense of sensory experience Abstract thinking Thoughts about feelings

Reptilian and diencephalon

The brain stem has the survival functions related to respiration, temperature control, and basic levels of physical comfort. Above this structure is the diencephalon, which is responsible for the regulation of homeostasis within the body. Hormonal balance, metabolism, and automatic movement are regulated by this part of the brain. Most of the functions at this level take place outside of our conscious awareness. It is only when survival is threatened in some way that individuals become consciously aware of changes at this level. The thalamus is responsible for receiving sensory-based information from around the body and co-ordinates information that drives behaviour and attention. Memory circuits are held in this portion of the brain, and develop as associated synaptic connections holding both visual and auditory information.

The basal ganglia determine instinctive responses, including will power. Activation of this area of the brain will result in stimulation of the autonomic nervous system, providing movement and action. These responses become generalized over time, and an element of choice is experienced on how to react based on past experience. Damage to this area of the brain is shown to directly affect the ability to learn through generalization and the development of habits (Mace, 2004). The basal ganglia holds sensory information related to pleasure and reward. Hypo-activity in this area results in a lack of thinking in relation to motivation that is directly related to pleasure and reward in response to external stimuli. Hyperactivity in this area may result in paranoid or manic processes, where motivational drives may become hyper-aroused. Obsessive–compulsive disorder (OCD) is also thought to arise from hyper-stimulation of this area (Goleman, 2003).

Basic motivational needs are stimulated by the hypothalamus within its primary role of regulating endocrine, motor, and autonomic functioning. These motivations are driven by internal signals of homeostasis and, where the balance is threatened, the body will react with both away from and towards motivational behaviours. Stress hormones are released through the body, which activates the sympathetic nervous system, moving us to action. Hyper-stimulation of this area can result in risk-taking behaviours or overt displays of aggression, whereas hypo-stimulation of this area can result in dissociation and detachment from meaning in life. To maintain equilibrium, the body will seek the early childhood patterning responses that have been neurologically connected in this area of the brain.

Palaeomammalian brain, or limbic system

The limbic system is responsible for making sense of the sensory motor information that is received through the reptilian brain. Motivational drives within this area of the brain are emotionally driven, and in under-developed brains, behaviours will be impulsive and reactionary, leading the person towards greater pleasurable reward or away from painful or distressing situations. Emotional meaning is held in this area of the brain, and permanent patterns of behaviour are set up in response to the emotional meaning that is laid down in early childhood. Anxiety and fear are neurologically linked in the amygdala, within the limbic system, and it is early childhood anxiety responses that later forms generalized and instinctive responses to anxiety-provoking situations in the future. This is the repetitive anxiety state seen in clients with attachment problems. Damage to this area of the brain is thought to affect the ability to trust and also to recognize and empathize with anxiety, fear, or sadness in others. They may also participate in risk-taking behaviours (Cozolino, 2002, LeDoux, 1998, Schore, 2003a,b).

The hippocampus acts as a regulator for the amygdala, providing discrimination for emotional responses to events. Learning occurs in this area of the brain, enabling an individual to differentiate between fear-producing situations and similar situations that do not produce fear. Hyper-stimulation of this area can affect the ability to differentiate between stressful and non-stressful situations, resulting in clients experiencing cross-contextual responses such as stress, phobia, and anxiety. Damage to this area of the brain can also affect short-term memory and the ability to recall previous learning situations.

The neomammalian brain

This part of the brain regulates voluntary muscle control, impulses, and plans for action, the interpretation of complex emotions, development and interpretation of symbols, and the drawing of logical conclusions from sensory motor and emotional stimuli.

The cingulate gyrus controls the ability to sense and interpret pain in self and others and is the structure that allows empathy and rapport with others. Stimulation of this area in infants will result in separation anxiety and crying (LeDoux, 1998). It is in this area of the brain that attachment responses are regulated, and when this is purposeful the child can move to a state of play and connection with others. Damage to this area of the brain can result in lack of ability to empathize with others and, depending on the particular area of the brain affected, may also affect the ability to think coherently.

The parietal lobes extend throughout each of the layers of the brain and are responsible for developing a sense of self in relation to others. Damage to this area of the brain affects the perception of the self in the world.

The insula is responsible for visceral sensations as well as an intuitive feeling response. Pain impulses arise in this part of the brain and the insula is responsible for interpreting these impulses and making meaning of these experiences. Damage to this area can result in lack of empathy for pain in others. The insula is also thought to be the domain of mirror neurons and the ability to perceive pain in others by feeling it in ourselves. Neglect is thought to directly influence the development of this area of the brain, caused by dissociation from an associated process.

The prefrontal cortex is responsible for maintaining emotional stability, converting all sensory stimuli into multiple layers of meaning and context, leading to abstract thinking and an ability to alter thought and action based on sensory input. Self reflection occurs in the prefrontal cortex, as does the ability to hold and perceive events through time as well as atemporally. Damage to the outer layers can affect cognitive functioning, whereas damage to the deeper layers will affect emotional functioning. Damage elsewhere in the brain will also affect the functioning of the prefrontal cortex (Goldberg, 2001).

The orbitofrontal cortex enables the adaptation of emotional responses and responding appropriately to the body's state in relation to the external environment. It is this area of the brain that is thought to be responsible for object permanence, a key element within secure attachment relationships. It is thought that this area of the brain also contains mirror neurons and the ability to mimic others' behaviour, a key step in psychosocial development. Damage to this area of the brain results in loss of emotional response and an inability to regulate behaviour in stressful situations. This can lead to inappropriate responses.

The dorsolateral prefrontal cortex is the action orientation aspect of higher cognitive functioning, including the ability to interpret multiple layers of emotional and cognitive information, make decisions, and then take action. This area of the brain has the ability to think in abstract concepts and make sense of internally generated images and symbols. Damage to this area of the brain can result in difficulty in focusing attention, action planning, and goal setting.

Developmental theory

Damasio (1994) observed that rather than each structure being built upon the previous one, each of the layers within the brain grew out of each other, and that all are entirely related and dependent on the others. Gerhardt (2004) has developed the work of Damasio and MacLean, among others, and proposes that the social brain or thinking brain can only develop in relation to others. We literally determine who we are and how we feel by focusing on, and making sense of, our external relationships. Gerhardt references Chugani's work (p. 38), who discovered that Romanian orphans who had been left in isolated conditions had a black hole where the orbitofrontal cortex should be.

It is between six and twelve months of age that primary attachment relationships are formed. There is an increased synaptic growth to the prefrontal cortex at this time, which is enabled through an infant's response to facial stimuli, particularly where positive looks are given. In response to the look, the infant experiences pleasurable sensations, resulting in a movement towards the pleasurable stimuli and a strong attachment bond is formed. Schore (2003a) suggests that this non-verbal communication and response to visual stimuli, including mirroring of facial expression, enables right brain to right brain communication, resulting in positive regulation of the right hemisphere. The right hemisphere is directly linked to the autonomic nervous system, responsible for regulation of sympathetic and parasympathetic responses.

In attachment disorder, it is thought that pruning has occurred between the synapses that connect the prefrontal cortex and the amygdala, or emotion-bearing centres of the brain, resulting in the experiencing of feelings that cannot be rationalized. In infants, it is the release or suppression of cortisol that determines the level of synaptic connection to the prefrontal cortex. A negative external response may result in a shift from the sympathetic to the parasympathetic nervous system and a resultant shut-down in emotional response. Additionally, when an infant (or an adult) is in a distressed state, a cognitive non-emotional response can also have a negative effect, resulting in emotional shut-down and distancing. Where there have been periods of time with reduced levels of cortisol, often through lack of empathy with the child, emotional abuse, and/or neglect, the child will respond with dissociation and may develop an avoidant attachment pattern.

Where an infant has experienced prolonged periods of time with raised cortisol levels, this can result in brain cells dying off. High cortisol levels are often found in clients with resistant attachment history, who may present with histories of anxiety, depression, suicidal ideation, addictive disorders, and/or histories of sexual abuse. It is possible to lower cortisol levels through self care, meditation, and relaxation processes, and alterations to diet and lifestyle.

Development of the brain continues through life, although there are major areas of activity up until the age of seven and then again leading up to the age of fifteen as the adolescent emerges through puberty. Recent theories in neuroscience have suggested that brain plasticity continues throughout life if the optimum conditions are present. The brain structures appear to become more rigid, with the neurobiological processes remaining fluid through life. This is clearly seen in the use of chemical neurobiological management of depressive disorders, where prescribed medication can alter the mood state of a client with endogenous depression. Within the therapy context, it is the processes of combining learning, emotional processing, and rationalization of emotional states, cortisol flow, and right brain to right brain communication that can aid brain plasticity and potential for growth and repair. Neural Darwinism, the ability to prune out synapses that are no longer required, combined with experience-dependent plasticity defined by Chugani

(1996) and Greenough and Black (1992), enables therapists to develop the ideal conditions for change.

A case of developmental delay

I first met Louise when she attended a training programme that I was co-teaching. She had already made connection with me prior to the course to ask about some pre-course reading. As soon as I entered the room, I felt an overpowering emotion, and, although there were several people in the room, it was clear that this was emanating from Louise. She introduced herself to me, and I managed to contain my countertransferential response appropriately to ensure that I could facilitate the training.

Some months after completing the day's training, Louise contacted me to ask if she could see me for therapy. I had no ongoing training relationship with her, so agreed that I would consider it after an assessment session.

At the assessment session, Louise explained why she had asked to see me. She was obsessed with the idea of getting cancer, and viewed every symptom that she had as indicative of cancer. Her uncle had died the previous year of cancer, and she described her thoughts as always going to the worst-case scenario, particularly if it involved her mother, husband, or children. She had been married for seven years and had two children. Her children were well and healthy, and although she had experienced difficult births, she had recovered well and had been able to breastfeed. She reported being continually anxious with her two children, and now that her son had started nursery school, she lived in fear that the phone would ring, telling her that something disastrous had happened.

Louise's early history was as an only child of parents who were in a difficult relationship. Her father had asked her mother to get rid of the baby as he did not want it cluttering up his life, and he left before she was born. He returned to the family home when she was three, and stayed for a few years, before twice leaving when Louise was at the ages of eight and twelve. When her father was at home, he would often bring other women into the house, and her mother would then leave the home and she would be left with her father. Her mother tried to kill herself when she was eight, and

Louise was sent to live with her uncle for a few months; this was the uncle who had died recently. She reports occasions when she asked her mum for a cuddle, who would then tell her to go away and leave her alone. She describes how her mother would regale her with tales of how abusive her father had been when they were married. She found it very difficult to get attention from her mother when she was growing up, and she quickly married when she left home. Louise's first marriage was to a violent man, who abused her sexually and physically. The marriage lasted six months before she left. She then remained on her own before getting married again to her current husband, who is emotionally distant, although there is no violence within the marriage.

Louise's relationship with her mother continues to be co-dependent, with Louise regularly giving up aspects of her life to help her mother in different ways. Her mother has also intruded on the marriage, and arguments have occurred with Louise feeling caught between her mother and her husband.

I have seen Louise intermittently for therapy over three years. Her presentation is one of disorganized attachment, and she tends to seek therapy when she becomes dysregulated and unpredictable. She has sufficient insight to know when she needs to be in therapy. My therapeutic approach has been a combination of psychodynamic and NLPt; it has not been possible or appropriate to maintain a brief therapy relationship with Louise. Where I have tried to contain it to brief interventions, this has created extreme anxiety in Louise, who has oscillated between being very angry with me to being very attached. At times, she has found it difficult to cope with lack of contact, and in the last few months of therapy, we were able to discuss and work with her attachment relationship to me. She has begun to transfer some of her insight into this to managing her relationship with her mother. Although her symptoms are minimal and she has a functional relationship with her husband, she still has difficulties with unpredictable behaviour, particularly when something occurs that triggers responses from her early childhood. As my therapy with her reduced in frequency, she developed transitional relationships to enable her to move towards greater self reliance. She has now changed her career and is working closely with a peer group to ensure that she contains and manages her affect in more appropriate ways.

CHAPTER FOUR

Creating potential for repair and growth in the brief therapies

With contributions from Betty Alice Erickson

The recent advances in neuroscience have enabled an understanding of the potential for repair and growth of neural synapses in psychotherapy work. Yet, it is clear that we are only just beginning to scratch the surface of what can be done within the therapy context. Many of the brief therapies include elements of neuroscience, and certainly some of them are able to provide empirical evidence of their effectiveness in working with a range of psychological disorders.

In this chapter, I summarize the main brief therapies and review the potential of neurological growth and repair that exists within each of them.

The chapter concludes with a contribution from Betty Alice Erickson, Milton Erickson's daughter. Betty Alice is a licensed Professional Counsellor, Marriage and Family Therapist, and works in private practice in Texas. She has authored numerous books and articles on Ericksonian therapy, and in this chapter, she summarizes Erickson's work with children with anxiety disorders.

Cognitive analytic therapy

CAT is already beginning to demonstrate its effectiveness in working with borderline states (Ryle, 1995a,b; Ryle & Beard, 1993). Borderline personality disorder (BPD) is a way of being in the world where the sense of self and the other is fragile, distorted, or fractured. The *DSM-IV* (2000) criteria defines this as a pervasive pattern of instability of interpersonal relationships, self image, and affects, with marked impulsivity beginning by early adulthood.

Some clients may be in a permanent borderline state, whereas others experience this state transiently. The client experiences vulnerability and anxiety that results in regression to earlier ways of coping and manipulation of perceptions. These defence mechanisms are recognized in psychoanalytic literature as the false self described by Winnicott (1960), the schizoid state described by Fairbairn (1946), and, more recently, the narcissistic states of Kernberg (1975) and Kohut and Wolf (1978). Gomez (1997) suggests that borderline states may be "the growing edge of maturation; even a small advance in our ability to contain and manage our feelings represents the reclaiming of experience from the rule of infantile processes" (p. 203).

Borderline states are subjective according to the observer, and any clinical diagnosis should be made in the context of experience, self-exploration of the therapist's perception and response to the client, and an awareness of social and medical models of control. Borderline states may occur with other psychopathologies, such as eating disorders, addictions, self harm, and para-suicidal tendencies.

In the context of attachment disorders, insecure and disorganized attachment patterns are considered to be linked to BPD (Fonagy et al., 1995), as has a history of maternal depression (Cole-Dekte & Kobak, 1994; Lyons-Ruth, Connell, Grunebaum & Botein, 1990; Murray & Cooper, 1997; and Radke-Yarrow, Cummings, Kuczinski, & Chapman, 1985).

CAT works with the internalized object and perception of self, and the self in relation to the other, enabling clients to understand and manage their own self-limiting beliefs and emotional states. The therapist works with transference and countertransference, and brings these unconscious processes into a dialogical and structured process of tasking within the therapy.

From a neuroscience perspective, links are made between the primitive emotional reflexes within the reptilian brain and diencephalon, the limbic system of learnt emotional responses, and the interpretation and understanding of sensory and emotional experience.

Ryle developed CAT therapy as a way of accessing and working with the deeper cognitive structures. Three constructs are considered within CAT:

- the dilemmas that a client is presented with where clients can often see only limited behavioural choice, the primary function of the basal ganglia within the limbic system;
- the traps or patterns of behaviour that reinforce negative perceptions of the self, a function of the prefrontal cortex;
- the snags or avoidance mechanisms that prevent change occurring, which may be concerning fear around goal activation, within the limbic system.

Through the process of therapy and gaining narrative understanding of their current lived experience, the client is encouraged to reformulate the patterns of his or her life in more useful ways.

By focusing on goals in therapy and linking these to the previous patterns of behaviour, it is possible that new neurological pathways are set up at a cognitive emotional level.

Cognitive–behavioural therapy (CBT)

Childhood trauma and attachment patterns are held within the right hemisphere of the brain, which is the centre for emotional connections, image forming symbolism, meaning, and non-cognitive processes. CBT focuses on the conscious experience of meaning making. In its early history, cognitive therapy utilized operant conditioning theories of Skinner (1961) and Pavlov (1927) to assist change of conditioned and automatic responses. In more recent years, there has been a move away from working with conditioned emotional and behavioural responses as more protocol driven therapy is required by the NHS. CBT has at its core the aim of enabling the client to develop an understanding of the relationship between thoughts, feelings, and behaviour, with the client focusing on here and now representations of the problem state. The process of therapy enables conscious and cognitive awareness of the problem state, and will use cognitive understanding as a means to address emotional or somatically held processes. The therapy is predominantly goal orientated, with set strategies, timescales, and goals for attainment of new skills and ways of responding. Where clients have effective functioning, this can be an efficient way of resolving unuseful behavioural patterns, as demonstrated in some of the research produced.

It is worth considering which aspects of the client's neurology is utilized in each of the assumptions that underpin CBT (Moorey, in Dryden, 1996, p. 256).

- The person is seen as an active agent who interacts with his or her world. This assumes an active and owned sense of self which, in clients without early trauma and neurological disturbance, is an empowering and useful assumption to make. It focuses the client on the more cognitive aspects of themselves and encourages the development of synaptic strength in the prefrontal and orbitofrontal cortex.
- This interaction takes place through the interpretations, inferences and evaluations that the person makes about his or her environment. This also focuses the client on the cognitive aspects of themselves, accessing the prefrontal and orbitofrontal cortex. It is unclear how this would enable an individual who has a fragmented or dissociated sense of self.
- The results of the "cognitive" processes are thought to be accessible to consciousness in the form of thoughts and images, and so the person has the potential to change them. This process focuses on the more advanced neomammalian brain structures. Yet symbolism and images are held within the diencephalon as visual and auditory images of primary experience. It is only if the person has developed an integrated sense of self that these can then be accessed through conscious processing.

CBT has a robust evidence base to support its place within the management of anxiety disorders. Chronic anxiety is a subcortical response, where the amygdala is self-activated (Panksepp, 1998). This occurs independently of cognitive functioning, and clients report distress at their apparent irrational anxiety reaction. CBT offers processes of respiratory control through self-administered breathing exercises, which result in a return to homeostasis within the limbic structures of the brain and a subsequent reduction in anxiety symptomatology. CBT is also useful for managing some elements of depressive disorder where there is an underlying anxiety state, and also OCD and contextual phobias. Goleman (2003) proposes that it is hyper stimulation of the basal ganglia that can occur in OCD, and by enabling focus to move to the more cognitive structures of the brain, this returns the basal ganglia to a less stimulated state.

CBT may also work by using cognitive structures to manage anxiety states and an increase in stimulation of the parasympathetic arousal response. This can be done through the relaxation techniques taught within CBT that are also found in many of the other forms of brief therapy, including NLPt, Ericksonian therapy and self relations therapy.

Inevitably, the move towards computerized CBT and bibliotherapy will deny any possibility of repair of early attachment problems, or where there is an undifferentiated sense of self, as the client no longer has access to the therapist for repair of these very early bonding and psychosocial development processes.

Eye movement desensitization and reprocessing (EMDR)

EMDR is probably one of the most effective methods, within the brief therapies, of enabling neurological repair and reprocessing in attachment and related disorders. There is a substantial evidence base of the effectiveness of EMDR in PTSD, arising from early trauma and attachment difficulties. PTSD is a psycho-neurological condition involving the reliving of traumatic experiences through all of the sensory motor, autonomic, sympathetic, flight/fright responses that cause avoidance or freezing behaviour, dissociation, or flooding of emotional responses. The body literally reacts as if the danger is reoccurring, and the client is unable to interrupt the conditioned response. PET scans have demonstrated reduced flow in the linguistic areas of the left hemisphere of the brain in clients experiencing PTSD and increased flow into the right limbic and parietal limbic system and the visual cortex (van der Kolk et al., 1996).

de Zulueta (2002, pp. 60–61) references the effectiveness of this approach in her work at the Maudsley Hospital. Research has demonstrated rapid results in 12–24 sessions using EMDR, and de Zulueta notes that the approach is particularly effective where the client has somatized responses of dysfunction or has difficulty recalling experiences. It is also considered to be helpful in situations where the client tends to over intellectualize their experience.

EMDR works by accessing memories that are held within the neural networks of the body. The memories may consist of thoughts, emotions, sensations, feelings, and visual flashbacks. It is thought that the memories are held as stuck states because the processing of the memory is incomplete, which may be because of unresolved resolution of the emotions or because dissociation and splitting occurred during the traumatic event. EMDR works on the principle that the solution state already exists within the neurology and that it is just functionally detached from the problem state. A conditioned response then arises in the body where any trigger that reminds the client of the original event will automatically cause a recurrence of the memory.

Of the five components that make up EMDR (Shapiro, 2001), each of these directly affect or influence different components of the neurological network and brain structures.

- Linking memory components through visualization processes enables the activation of neural synapses within the thalamus in the brain stem. The thalamus holds primary visual and auditory memory. At the same time, visualization activates the higher cognitive structures of the brain that are responsible for making sense of meaning from a combination of sensory motor, emotional, and cognitive stimuli. By focusing on the visual image of the event, the neural connection between the original primary input in the reptilian structures is directly linked to the cognitive structures, enabling rationalization of the experience.

- Mindfulness enables the client to witness from within his/her own cognitive structures a reliving of the experience from a dissociated observer stance, enabling this learning to recontextualize the event.

- Free association encourages the client to set up experience-dependent brain plasticity (Greenough, Black, & Wallace, 1987) by allowing the observation and reporting of new associations that occur during the session. This processing of new learning enables the development of new neural pathways to existing resource states within the client.

- Repeated access to, and dismissal of, traumatic imagery also enables experience-dependent brain plasticity to occur as the client experiences rapid association and dissociation into the negative state. When traumatic events are re-accessed, the amygdala becomes activated causing stress arousal and a fear response. By triggering the prefrontal cortex at the same time through dismissing the imagery, the triggered response experienced within the amygdala then collapses and the neurological connection disappears.

- Eye movements, hand tapping, and auditory stimuli provide accessing of different synaptic connections through the diencephalon and limbic brain structures, freeing memories held within deeper unconscious neurological networks.

Ericksonian therapy

Erickson began his work as a therapist before attachment theory was developed by Bowlby. In his early career as a psychiatrist, he viewed psychological symptoms from an analytic perspective, and it was only as his interest in hypnosis and the positive potential within unconscious processing grew, in the 1960s, that he developed a view of neurosis as predominantly protective and defensive (Short, Erickson, & Erickson Klein, 2005). Erickson considered that people need to feel secure within their own bodies, and the focus of his therapy was to encourage and develop an awareness of this goodness and sense of security within the self, removing the focus of attachment problems from the other to the self (*ibid.*, p. 30). He also operated from a principle of leaving unconscious that which needed to remain unconscious, rather than flooding the client's cognitive structures with traumatic memories. Amnesia through hypnosis was an important part of this therapeutic strategy, and he would approach the resolution of childhood trauma through a process of progressive desensitization where he would utilize symbols and the client's own rate of progress to enable gradual cognitive assimilation of traumatic experiences.

Erickson had an innovative and unusual approach to therapy, which would sometimes continue outside of the traditional therapy setting. He regularly tasked clients from a systemic stance (Rosen, 1992), conducting therapy outside of the session, and would also, on occasions, develop and utilize life-long attachments with his clients (Short, Erickson, & Erickson Klein, 2005). He utilized himself in the therapy, particularly in the use of indirect suggestion. He found that he was able to assist clients to resolve their early child-hood relationship with their mother by talking about his own mother (Erickson, in Short, Erickson, & Erickson Klein, 2005).

Ericksonian approaches consist of six core strategies of thera-peutic intervention (*ibid.*).

- Distraction of the conscious mind to facilitate unconscious change. In Ericksonian therapy, the focus is on the preferred future for the client, based on existing and currently under-utilized existing resources. Erickson utilized abstraction in metaphor (Rosen, 1992) to enable activation of the cognitive search for meaning to become directly neurologically linked to the problem state. By chunking up in levels of abstraction, the client would be required to map across solution states to the existing problem state.
- Partitioning, which may enable association into more manage-able components of the problem state. Rather than addressing the problem state in its entirety, the focus is to assist in making more manageable acceptance of the problem state by focusing on one aspect of the problem at a time. This moves the client from a state of being overwhelmed, and the amygdala responding with hyper stimulation and emotional flooding, to being able to cognitively process small components at a point in time. Partitioning can also be assisted through combined elements of association and dissociation, and shifting of the temporal perspective (Erickson & Rossi, 1989).
- Progression follows partitioning and, as one aspect of the neurology is freed from the problem state, development is encouraged in this area. This may be through cognitive tasking, reframing, or the use of unconscious suggestions of change.
- Suggestion of the possibility of change. An Ericksonian ap-proach combines elements of indirect and permissive linguistic

patterns and elements of choice, creating the both / and position within the cognitive structures activating the basal ganglia and the prefrontal cortex at the same time. The basal ganglia controls will and basic choices about survival whereas the prefrontal cortex determine the actions to take based on sensory motor input.

• Reorientation by providing an alternative perspective. This process can only occur when sufficient rapport is present between the therapist and the client. This opens up potential within the cingulate gyrus, which is the structure that enables rapport and empathy with others. Reorientation can also occur by providing a temporal perspective to the change, activating the prefrontal cortex and the ability to self reflect (Erickson & Rossi, 1989)

• Utilization and positive acknowledgement of the more shameful aspects of the self, leading to validation of the client and an increase in sense of self. As the client represents the more shameful or distressing aspects of themselves, this causes a release of neural transmitters from the subcortex, activating the synaptic connections of the problem state. By the therapist accepting, validating, and utilizing these aspects, the presence of stress hormones within the subcortex, and the resultant connection to the higher cognitive centres, will set up new neural synapses in response to this validation of the self.

Neurolinguistic psychotherapy

NLPt is an outcome-orientated psychotherapy that works with the neurolinguistic reality of a client's subjective experience of the world. As it is a therapy that is primarily here and now based, and is focused towards client outcomes; it does not place great emphasis on the past and attachment-based relationships. It does, however, offer a considerable potential for working with neurological processing and the resultant linguistic representations of a client's inner world.

NLPt operates from a number of philosophical principles known as presuppositions (Dilts & DeLozier, 2000), some of which are relevant to attachment-based problems.

- Mind-and-body form a cybernetic system. By communicating with one aspect of the client's system, it is possible to directly influence other aspects. This links to the Ericksonian approach of partitioning and progression described above (Chopra, 1989; Pert, 1997).
- The processes that take place within a person and between people and their environment are systemic. Our bodies, our societies, and our universe form an ecology of systems and subsystems, all of which interact with, and mutually influence, each other *and* a pattern of associations (anchors) may be set up through a single trial experience in contrast to linear repetitions (Skinner, 1961).
- At some level, all behaviour is (or was at one time) "positively intended" *and* people make the best choices available to them given the possibilities and capabilities that they perceive available to them from their model of the world (Haley, 1973; Rogers, 1951). It is possible to acknowledge difficulties that a client is experiencing and utilize them in a positive way to facilitate change.
- People already have (or potentially have) all of the resources they need to act effectively. Rothschild (2000) suggests that we have five major classes of resources: functional, physical, psychological, interpersonal, and spiritual (pp. 88–92). Rothschild (*ibid.*) proposes that finding the opposite of a defence mechanism creates choice and balance as well as a potential resource.

NLPt has a number of processes within the methodology that can be utilized to enhance neurological functioning.

- Rapport is a process of matching the unconscious behaviours of another to facilitate unconscious acceptance of verbal and non-verbal suggestions that are offered to it. It facilitates right brain to right brain communication, and has been demonstrated to successfully activate mirror neurons (Gallese, 2001; Gallese & Goldman, 1998; Gallese, Fadiga, Fogassi, & Rizzolatti, 1996; Rizzolatti, Fadiga, Fogassi, & Gallese, 1999).
- Sensory acuity is awareness of the moment-to-moment changes that occur in the client as they make shifts between the

sympathetic and parasympathetic nervous system. This can be utilized to facilitate association and dissociation in the client, ensuring that the client can be dissociated from negative emotions that can cause hyper-stimulation of the amygdala, and association into positive emotions and experiences, which can lead to the collapse of unuseful neural pathways.

- Outcome setting links directly to the motivational elements of the hypothalamus and the limbic system

- Submodalities are the subcoding elements within the primary representational systems of visual, auditory, kinaesthetic, olfactory, and gustatory components of the nervous system. It is these finer distinctions that enable the coding, ordering, and meaning of experience. One of the submodalities that is most relevant to working with attachment-related states is association and dissociation. It is possible to alter associate states (and vice versa) by altering the finer distinctions of internal imagery. Further information on this is provided in Chapter Five.

- Strategies provide a description of the internal and external sequence of representations that produce a specific outcome. Each step within a strategy will consist of submodality distinctions and will be made up of sensory and non-sensory information. By altering the strategy, it is possible to alter the behavioural response in a given situation. This process links the cognitive and emotional processing centres of the brain.

- Language patterns of abstract and detailed thinking provide clues to the client's inner world. It also provides the potential to influence the chunking and sorting of information, particularly within processes of solution activation through abstract language patterns that will trigger higher order cognitive functioning. Linguistic processes can also be used to bypass conscious levels of resistance and access unconscious resource states.

- Eye patterns are one of the components of NLP that aid understanding of cognitive thought processes. They can also be utilized in a similar way to the process of eye movement within EMDR through a technique known as new behaviour generator (Dilts & Epstein, 1991).

- Anchoring is the basis of operant conditioning and conditioned responses (Pavlov, 1927; Skinner, 1961). By anchoring resourceful states accessed through recalled positive memories held within the thalamus, the neuronal circuits are activated. If these are neurologically activated at the same time as negative memory states held in the same region of the brain, this can cause a collapse of the negative neural pathway into the more positively charged neural pathway.

- Reframing provides the opportunity to relearn and reframe experiences as they are emotionally held within the hippocampus, by linking these experiences to more effective and rationalized forms of meaning in the higher cognitive structures.

- Parts integration is a process of aligning or integrating dissociated aspects of the personality to become functionally connected with the more resourceful adult self. Through a process of association, dissociation, and re-association, and chunking up to find common cognitive intent behind the behaviour, it is possible to reintegrate these more fragmented and regressed aspects of the personality (Gilligan, 1997; James, 2003; O'Hanlon & Bertolino, 1998).

- Time lining is a process of temporal reframing that enables the deactivation of emotionally intense gestalts within the neurology. Temporal reframing directly activates and alters the sense of self in relation to emotion and meaning within the prefrontal cortex, moving the client to a state of emotional stability.

- Symbolic modelling has emerged out of NLPt and was co-developed by Lawley and Tomkins (2005) following their modelling of the metaphor work of David Grove. Symbolic modelling enables the representation of non-linguistic and non-linear representations of experience, bringing together neurological connections that transcend throughout the brain structures.

- Values alignment provides a comprehensive process of understanding motivational traits and influences, including processes of pattern recognition. Activation of the hypothalamus and limbic structures occurs directly in response to values-based work, and alignment of values involves integration and assimilation of "away from" behaviours.

Provocative therapy

Provocative therapy is a form of psychotherapy that can create results with a client who is willing to own and work with his own self-defeating behaviours. Having fun and laughter is a key element of this therapy, and, as such, provides a social attachment function. There is a direct correlation between separation pain mechanisms, attachment, and affective exchanges (Hart, 2008, p. 188).

Within the recognized processes of PT, some aspects have direct correlations to areas of neurological processing, whereas others act as direct contraindications for working with clients with complex attachment problems, particularly where borderline states may become activated.

- Ongoing behaviours of non-verbal mirroring will activate mirror neurons, and the intense focus on the client may replicate the early gaze process that is considered to be essential in developing positive attachment relationships (Schore, 2003a, pp. 7–15).
- Conditional behaviours, such as activating the emotion, causing a stress response in the amygdala, which is then responded to seriously, offering the client a sense of validation.
- Provocative tools and reactions to problem states can result in right brain misattunement, which is triggered by mismatching and can result "in a stressful desynchronisation between and destabilisation with the right brain" (Schore, 2003a, pp. 51–52), and, where this process is used, rapid reattunement must follow in vulnerable clients.
- Therapists'/consultants' internal processes, which are similar to those of a caring mother/parent figure, of warmth, and happiness. Each of these aspects will enable empathic resonance.

Rational emotive behaviour therapy (REBT)

REBT is similar in some processes to CBT; however, the primary purpose of therapy is an integrated sense of self that includes emotional as well as behavioural components. REBT focuses on the motivational aspects of a client's internal world and directly attunes with the hypothalamus and limbic system. Cognitive awareness of motivational traits is raised within the client's cognitive processes, enabling the rationalization of the less rational motivational impulses that prevent the client from achieving what they hope to achieve.

REBT holds the view that irrational beliefs are distortions of perception. Stern (1998) refers to distortions as the subjective view being distorted from the objective reality. Positive distortions of the self in early infancy can lead to an integrated and positive sense of self with a positive future outlook. Negative distortions of the self can occur where there have been negative projections on to the child in infancy that later become internal working models of the self in relation to others.

REBT works to alter the internal distorted model of the self through a series of processes that enable integration of irrational beliefs and resultant emotional states. Many of the principles identified by Froggat (1997) would be limited or non-existent in clients with poor attachment histories, leading to an ineffective life. In considering the prerequisites identified by Dryden (1996) for therapy to be effective, there are a number of processes that can be aided through greater understanding of neuropsychological processes.

- Outcome orientation. Similar to Ericksonian therapy, NLPt, and provocative therapy, the outcome-orientated nature of this approach will directly activate the hypothalamus and limbic systems.
- Therapy is strictly time limited, which may affect the ability to gain therapeutic empathy and resonance through right brain to right brain attunement, particularly where clients may require a longer time frame to experience a positive attachment relationship. Evidence of a good working bond between therapist and client is required from the outset.
- The individual is required to target two specific problems within the therapy. This process provides a sense of containment for the client, and also a partitioning of problem states to ensure that they are manageable with the time frame given.
- Cognitive commitment to the tasking within REBT is required, and provides direct connection to the higher cognitive structures. This may create a sense of urgency for the client and activation of the synaptic connections within the hippocampus, enabling choices to be made and differentiation between stressful and non-stressful events.

Self relations therapy

Of the brief therapies described, self relations therapy is probably the one that most closely matches the triunal brain and respondent processes that mirror the neurological processing within each of the brain structures. Gilligan operates from a principle of considering positive and negative changes in state as providing potential for personal growth, repair, and development. His ground-breaking therapy stays away from direct links to neuroscience; however, his descriptions of the individual moving through cycles of death and rebirth as new identities are formed provides an effective description of ongoing plasticity of brain functions. Hart (2008) proposes that the more the brain is used, the more neurons communicate with each other, and the easier it is for new learning to take place. Gilligan's approach of constantly reframing and utilizing negative states for positive benefit leads to an integrated sense of self and greater potential for growth.

The somatic mind provides a description of the diencephalons, with the primary function of responding to survival instincts. Gilligan expands on this ability, and suggests that this is the basic function and that a secondary, and more generative, function is also held within this mind, that of the ability to hold and contextualize emotional experiences. Gilligan refers to the accessing of this state of mind as one of centring, where the client focuses on a positive, felt sense of self, and utilizes this state of equilibrium to manage experiences of stress and trauma. It is likely that this process of holding awareness of the primary stress response within the diencephalon and choosing an alternative behavioural response through the insula and prefrontal cortex enables neurological connections to be made and an alternative synaptic response to be set up.

The cognitive mind, at a basic level, describes the lower functions of the neomammalian brain, whereas the generative mind in Gilligan's description describes the functions of the prefrontal, orbitofrontal, and dorsolateral prefrontal cortex. The sense of self in relation to others is held within the generative mind, which would suggest involvement of the parietal lobes, essential in developing positive attachment relationships.

The field or relational mind holds the self within constraints and boundaries at the current existing identity or pattern of behaviour.

The generative level enables transcendence beyond boundaries and moves the client beyond the problem to the space beyond. It is here that expanded awareness occurs. Gerhardt (2004) refers to this as the ability to generate openness, where feelings literally come and go, are witnessed and responded to appropriately, and are not held stuck in the body. This process also enables the regulation of self states in relation to others, the relational field.

In reviewing the six major premises of Gilligan's (2004) model, there are correlations to the neurological structures and processes described in Chapter Three.

- The centre is the diencephalon and the invisible presence of somatic knowing and experiencing is held in the insula, the visceral and intuitive responses.
- Flight, fight, and fright responses are held within the centre and SR therapy uses the connection of this centre to the higher cognitive structures to bring awareness of the contextualized meaning of somatically held responses.
- Accessing and allowing the emotions to flow through the body, rather than holding them in stuck frozen positions, results in the experiencing of both positive and negative events and emotions. By centring and gaining conscious awareness of the stress response, and then taking time to think before acting, new synaptic connections are set up, enabling new behavioural choice.
- There is a direct relationship between the cognitive and somatic self. This is likely to be via the parietal lobes, which extend throughout the brain structures and are responsible for developing a sense of self in relation to others, that is, the relational self.
- Harmonization of the two selves to develop a third relational self that has connections to the relational field. At some level, this includes a sense of security of the self in the world.
- Validation of the self supports Schore's (2003a) of empathic resonance.

Solution focused brief therapy (SFBT)

SFBT is a model of therapy that focuses only on possible solutions and preferred futures. The solution focused approach acknowledges and validates all the client's feelings and beliefs. It then asks about possible hopes and options, and then looks for instances of these already happening in the client's life, as well as any exceptions to the problem behaviours. Thus, it enables the accessing of resources within the client to have more of what they want (solution) and less of what they do not want (problem).

Gerhardt (2004) suggests that habits and generalized responses are difficult to change and can only be changed by doing them differently. By the therapist accepting and validating the emotions, the already activated stress hormones provide the potential to set up new neural signals within the higher brain with new ways of thinking and feeling. Hart (2008) expands on this, and links back to neural Darwinism, that the set up of new neural pathways will result in pruning of the old pathways, "Every new wave of neural organization dissolves the former organization, so there are inevitable periods of transition where the old approach no longer works while a new approach has not yet been established" (p. 76). This transitional process can be aided through the solution-focused approach.

Within SFBT, there are a number of assumptions that support the development of new ways of thinking. Although SFBT does not consider that repair is required, there are some processes that could enable neurological repair and growth in attachment related issues.

- There is an assumption of respect for the client, enabling resonance empathy and accessing of mirror neurons. This right brain to right brain communication has the potential for the formation of new attachment processes.
- The client has the ability to shape their lives; they have already set up patterns of ways of being and can equally set up new patterns.
- Therapy focuses on solutions and times when the problem does not happen. By bringing these solution states to consciousness, the client is able to activate further these synaptic connections. As these small successes are brought into awareness, the therapist encourages the client to repeat them, building up further synaptic strength. Because the solution is already inherent in the client and does not involve new ways of learning, just an expansion of existing ways of being, therapy is brief.

• By associating into a preferred future, a greater sense of self emerges, and the client's neurology becomes activated around the motivational and goal-setting areas of the current state, responding to pleasure rather than fear or pain.

Each session of SFBT commences with a set of questions that activate future-orientated neural synapses. These questions focus around the best hopes for the therapy; visual representation of what everyday life would look like if the hopes were realized. They cause a direct activation of the thalamus and basal ganglia, and activation of current processes that enable realization of the hopes, accessing the higher cognitive structures.

The process of SFBT leaves the client in charge of the therapy, assuming that the solution exists within the client. As the client considers alternative futures and best hopes, he may use visual representations of what this might look like. This process links the negative motivational patterns to more positive, visually represented ways of thinking and being.

Goal setting is a major component of SFBT, with time spent with the client developing a detailed description of the achievement of the goal. The goal is also chunked to manageable levels and is action based, linking the basal ganglia function of pleasure, reward, and action with the dorsolateral prefrontal cortex.

At subsequent sessions, the therapist commences the therapy with the question "What's better?" Immediately, the solution state is accessed and built on, enabling a strengthening of these synaptic connections and a further pruning of the old problem state.

Ericksonian therapy, contributed by Betty Alice Erickson

Milton Erickson practised his creative methods of psychotherapy long before attachment disorders were accepted diagnoses. Clearly, symptoms were present in many of the children and adults with whom Erickson worked. He knew the purpose of therapy was to create a better, more productive, and independent life, and his patients achieved this.

He believed in a secure reality for all children; he knew that if children were not certain that someone other than their small self was "in charge", their lives were filled with anxieties, typically handled by escalation of dysfunctional behaviours in attempts to find security. They also almost always demonstrated huge needs for control. Connection with other people always means some measure of vulnerability, so giving and receiving affection was sacrificed.

Erickson also pioneered using the patient's own non-productive behaviours as the vehicle for change. In that way, the patient had control, but that control was guided by impersonal and real-world consequences. Oppositional responses were not as necessary because the patient still felt he had control. He also believed that any change, no matter how minor it seemed, created a new reality for a patient, and new responses were then required.

A few case examples will illustrate.

Lucy

Erickson worked with a woman whose four-year-old foster child had great difficulty adjusting to her new home. Lucy not only had been abandoned by her parents, but her medical problems involved multiple uncomfortable treatments by hurried health-care professionals. Her only loving home had been short-term, and she had been removed with no understandable explanation.

Lucy coped with her new surroundings by controlling as much of her environment as she could. There were three older brothers in her home and, perhaps because of that, Lucy chose passive resistance rather than overt behaviours. For example, as she walked slowly, the family had to slow down. When she "forgot" how to get dressed, someone had to help her get dressed, or everyone had to wait. In discussions with Erickson, her mother realized Lucy had frequently refused to eat and had tried to get special foods prepared for her alone. But the mother had assumed that if Lucy didn't eat, she wasn't hungry; eating between meals was simply not an option in that home.

Erickson explained to the mother that Lucy—and most children with these behaviours—had lived through more punishments than adults could comprehend. Some of those punishments may have been inadvertent, but the child's needs were not met. That was perceived as a threat to autonomy, even to life, and Lucy was desperately trying, in a childish way, to get those needs met. If she could control, she would be safe. Therefore, Erickson emphasized, she could not be punished in "traditional" ways.

Even children understand that behaviours have consequences. Touch a hot stove and it burns. So, Erickson said, using Lucy's own behaviours to teach her more productive ways could not be seen as "punishment". The parents' problem, he emphasized, is that they want the child to have a better life. They want things to work out. They want the common ordinary parenting problems with an ordinary child. That seems absolutely normal to them, just as the child's need to protect his vulnerability by controlling and other acting out seems normal to him.

Using her behaviours as the consequence, Erickson said, was a way around her need for control. They decided that her habit of walking slowly was something that infuriated the whole family, so that was one first step, literally and figuratively, to begin changes in Lucy. He wanted Lucy's mother to praise her for her outstanding ability to walk slowly. Only she could walk so slowly, so gracefully. Everyone in the family should admire Lucy's ability to do this. If Lucy decided to walk faster, that was fine; if she did not, there was another level to the plan.

Two weeks later, Lucy's mother reported that the girl had walked normally a couple of times, but most of the time she continued her deliberate slow pace. The family had all truthfully admired her skill. She was the slow walker champion! It was like watching a slow-motion film! Lucy was clearly confused, but could not help but feel a bit of pride. Her brothers were puzzled, but knew parents frequently do puzzling things and were happy to join in the praise. Then Erickson laid out the next phase.

There was to be a Cookie Party. Mum would interrupt a game that Dad was participating in, for the children to each have a plate of cookies and glass of chocolate milk at their small lunch table. As they came in, Mother was to direct the boys to the table and say happily that Lucy could do what she was so good at doing. She got to walk SLOWLY while everyone watched and admired her slowness. It was important that this was framed as a genuine treat for Lucy; it was something she liked to do, that she was proud of doing. Her plate of cookies was there, waiting for her, while she walked slowly and everyone admired her championship ability!

Lucy walked slowly, and everyone admired her slow-motion movements. When she reached the table to sit down, her father announced matter-of-factly that the time allotted for the Cookie Party was over and removed the plates. Everybody could now go and play. The young boys had finished their treat, and raced outside. Lucy complained that she wanted her cookies. Her parents explained once again, that the time allotted for the Cookie Party was over. It was play time again. But she had demonstrated walking slowly! And everybody admired it!

Erickson emphasized that there could be not the slightest hint of punishment or "serves you right" in this interaction. The parents had to be earnestly sincere. Never forget the power of stupidity, Erickson often said. Those who "can't" often have a great deal of covert power.

Lucy's mother reported back that Lucy began to be angry, but she and the father stayed in the mode of confusion—it was a lovely little party, but now it was play time. Mum whisked Lucy outside, and Dad began tossing the ball to all four children, and everyone acted as though everything was normal, as it was.

Lucy learnt. She never deliberately walked slowly again. She had many other passive aggressive behaviours, all of which could be dealt with in similar creative ways.

Erickson helped Lucy's parents with much of her socialization and willingness to trust her new family. He was clear that Lucy very much needed a sense of control, as she had had virtually none in her entire life. But the parents also needed control, partly in order to create a secure reality for Lucy. Rules that were important were called "Rules of the House". Impersonal, everyone obeyed them. "In this house, we . . ." or we suffered the logical consequences. Everyone had to brush their teeth, everyone put their dishes in the dishwasher, everyone had to get dressed before breakfast. If Lucy didn't brush her teeth, someone helped her. This was not a punishment, it merely was. Mum and Dad had to be confused if someone didn't follow House Rules. There could be no punishing.

At one point, Lucy began refusing to get dressed in the mornings. She liked to eat breakfast in her nightclothes. The parents merely looked confused. They pointed out to Lucy that In This House, everyone had to get dressed before breakfast.

Lucy didn't care. She would skip breakfast and get dressed before lunch. The parents made a quick call to Erickson. He reiterated that Rules of the House had to be followed to the letter. The sun comes up in the east, sets in the west, and Rules of the House are followed. A new House Rule had to be established—In This House, first we eat breakfast, then we eat lunch, and then we eat dinner. If Lucy didn't eat breakfast, how could she eat lunch?

The parents followed Erickson's advice. The next morning when Lucy ambled into the dining room in her nightgown, they asked Lucy, with great confusion in their voices, how could she eat lunch? She hadn't had breakfast; the time for breakfast was long past. But, they said brightly, there was always tomorrow. And mother made sure to prepare Lucy's favourite food for dinner. Everyone was appropriately dismayed that Lucy had to skip dinner. Lucy learnt very quickly that impersonal Rules of the House were obeyed.

Erickson also helped the family to redefine control. Sometimes, the cost of control kept Lucy from her own happiness, and had no effect on others. For example, the family often had a backwards meal, and dessert was served before the dinner. If Lucy refused dessert because it was out of order, no one cared. Everyone in the family experimented with taking their showers with their socks. Sometimes, people got to sleep on top of their bed, and then they didn't have to make the bed up in the morning. Any adult can think of many other ways to turn unnecessary control into a game. That helps a child understand that control is not always necessary—and sometimes it is fun to let go of the need to control.

Years later, Lucy still has a need for control and has chosen a career that allows her to exercise that productively. She is in charge of inventories and supplies for a large company. She keeps track of all the supplies and re-orders when she deems necessary. Her boss thinks she is wonderful! Her department runs more smoothly and efficiently than ever!

Erickson consulted with this author (Betty Alice) when she was managing a small, self-contained school for delinquent teenagers. In retrospect, the youngsters were displaying symptoms of attachment disorders; many had been adopted, most had abusive childhoods. These children acted out in highly aggressive ways, as well as in passive withdrawing ways. The commonality of their acting out, the school counsellor and I both felt, was their desperate, though futile, attempts to control an unfriendly and threatening world. This, of course, created a loop: acting out guarantees unpleasant responses, which feeds into acting out even more. The same concepts were used. Not only did all behaviours have reasonable and expected consequences, both good and bad, but the teacher removed herself from the system. With the exception of three basic rules, each cause for immediate suspension or expulsion, the students were totally responsible for the operation of the school.

Kathy

One of our twenty-two students, Kathy, consistently acted out each Friday. She had few friends and was generally content being isolated. Schoolwork was structured, so she accomplished that. But on Fridays, she took home a "progress report", which included a behaviour report. Almost always she did something overtly destructive so her behaviour report had something terrible to say. Then her parents would punish her over the weekend—and it would start all over the next Monday. This pattern became clear even to the other students: she "liked" to get punished, to be grounded, to lose her privileges. Much as a child will hand a neighbour something he is uncertain about, saying, "I bet you won't like this," Kathy had the illusion of controlling her parents' responses to her over the weekend. She also "rescued" herself from the fears of closeness with them.

The counsellor and I discussed our options. He admired Erickson's work, so I asked my father for help. We told Erickson, that Friday was the only day Kathy acted out overtly. Perhaps she wanted to end the week on an unhappy note, thereby, perhaps, showing she still had damage. Perhaps she liked to disappoint herself and her parents by raising everyone's hopes once again, and then failing once again. Perhaps five days of consistency was too much for her.

The only thing we knew for sure was that we didn't know for sure. Erickson then helped us to change one piece of the picture— the one piece we had under our control. We all believed that if one part of a whole is changed, other elements have to change too. The next Monday, the counsellor and I announced we were doing something different, just for fun. We were bored with the same old routine of Monday, Tuesday, Wednesday, Thursday, and Friday. Then, per Erickson's paradigm, we entered distraction into the mix. We began talking about how many times in our lifetime we had followed that habitual pattern. We asked the students also figure out how many weeks they had lived through the monotonous sequence. Everyone, including Kathy, joined in.

We then told the students we were going to change this dull and repetitive sequence for us, and for our own special little school world. Today was officially Wednesday! Each student had to make a personal calendar changing the days around. Following Erickson's suggestion again, we distracted and bored with a lengthy explanation of how to mix up the remaining four days. The only rule was that they could not put any day in its "old" position.

The staff and students would work together to smooth out any difficulties. The students talked together with great good humour. Class schedules were rearranged. People who regularly saw the counsellor on Wednesdays appeared for their appointments and those who were supposed to be there on Monday were sent away. The switch in days seemed like an amusing twist for everyone. As the renamed Friday, approached, Kathy seemed oblivious to the underlying structure of this change. That day came and went uneventfully. Then the real Friday, the last day of the week approached. But it wasn't named Friday, and she herself had limited her destructiveness to Fridays. The counsellor and I waited to see if she would take the face-saving, and very safe, way out, to change, that had been offered her. We both believed the best part of her wanted to be a better person—she was just fearful of trying it on. Throughout the last day of the week, Kathy acted as she usually acted on other days.

Right before school was dismissed for the weekend, we held a short meeting. We liked the new and improved interesting schedule, we said. We would keep it in effect, at least for a while. Students could make new weekly calendars or they could keep the ones they'd already made. The extra-good news, the counsellor added, was that Ms Erickson had been so caught up in our new and exciting system that she had not got around to making any behaviour reports. Everyone knew how those kinds of things confused Ms Erickson, the counsellor went on, so it might take her a while to figure out anything. That seeded the possibility that if they made good changes, they would "force" me into making one, a change they desired, too. He finished by showing the notices he'd made for them to give their parents. It merely that stated no weekly reports were being issued.

It would be nice to say that this small change created enormous healing within the students, and with Kathy especially. It didn't, but it did make noticeable differences with everyone, especially Kathy. The days of the week were kept scrambled for three months until a week's vacation occurred. When we came back from vacation, we all "forgot" to re-do our special calendars.

Behaviour reports were not reinstituted for several weeks—mostly because the students behaved more appropriately. Kathy never received another weekly report of poor behaviour; she began responding in far more normal and appropriate ways. During the three months that we had "different days", not one student wanted to go back to the regular calendar. Some even took advantage of changing the days of the week on their calendar so they could have extra time to prepare for a test or project deadline and one creative lad changed the names of all the days to made-up words.

Healing of deep pain, deep injuries, take a long time. But every layer of healing adds substance to the person. Any way we could give the students suitable, proper, and earned power and control added to their healing.

CHAPTER FIVE

Outcome orientation as a model of psychotherapy

G oal orientation and outcome focus is a common component of each of the brief therapies described in this book. Each therapy approaches goals and outcomes differently, and some approaches will focus only on the outcome without referring to past related issues. This chapter reviews the outcome process of each brief therapy, and then considers stress and arousal responses in regulated and dysregulated individuals. The use of sensory motor stimuli and associated and dissociated states is discussed, leading to an understanding of motivational patterns and goal orientation.

Outcome processes in brief therapy

Cognitive analytic therapy acknowledges and works with past, present, and future states, with the aim being to create more effective ways of responding behaviourally and emotionally in the future.

Cognitive behavioural therapy operates in the here and now to gain insight into the relationship between thoughts, feelings, and behaviour. The approach includes clear strategies, goals, and timescales for developing psychological and/or behavioural skills. Goal orientation is in the immediate future.

Eye movement desensitization and reprocessing is also a here and now process that enables new learning and associations for the immediate future.

Ericksonian therapy accesses latent potential for here and now and future-orientated states. It assumes that the solution already exists and accesses this solution state for the immediate and longer-term future, enabling the client to gain hope of a better and more purposeful future.

Neurolinguistic psychotherapy is an outcome-orientated therapy based on what is possible for the client. It assumes success and involves the application of successful strategies to a future-orientated way of being. The purpose of therapy is to increase choice for a client and facilitate them to a more resourceful state than they currently have access to.

Provocative therapy focuses on the more positive aspects of the here and now, moving the client to a more hopeful future.

Rational emotive behaviour therapy is a goal-orientated therapy that focuses on immediate and longer-term goals that are rational, achievable, and realistic. It acknowledges the goal-seeking nature of human existence and the drive to survive and pursue happiness. The aim of therapy is to remove blockages that prevent the attainment of goals.

Self relations therapy is here and now and future orientated in process and assumption. The focus of therapy is the utilization of current states as opportunities for personal growth and development in the now and the future. The focus is on channelling positive and negative energies towards a preferred future.

Solution focused brief therapy assumes that all problems have the solution inherent within them. Therapy focuses only on solutions for the here and now, the immediate future, and the longer-term future. The aim of therapy is to assist the client to develop hope towards the future, which then becomes evolutionary, with the client's hope leading them to want to achieve more and becoming eager to build on past successes. All of the processes and questions within the therapy are outcome orientated. A preferred future that is specifically stated is a major focus for the therapy. Scaling processes are used to assist the client to access and move towards the preferred future.

Stress and arousal responses

The reticular activation system within the brain is responsible for arousal and motivation, circadian rhythm, respiratory and cardiac rhythms, and is considered to be the physical process that is responsible for Freud's "psychical energy" (Schore, 2003a, p. 225). The reticular activation system is directly influenced by stress and arousal responses, which are processed through the sympathetic and parasympathetic nervous system. These systems are fully present at birth, and the system develops mature functioning directly through the early care-giver relationship (Hart, 2008). This occurs through regulation of affective states, with the care-giver responding to right brain cues that indicate levels of stress and relaxation in the infant. Comprehensive descriptions of these processes are offered by Schore (2003a) and Gerhardt (2004).

Recent understandings in neuroscience have provided a level of insight into the stress response as it relates to rupture in the attachment relationship (Perry, Pollard, Blakely, Baker, & Vigilante, 1995). Homeostasis and a feeling of calm in an infant are enabled through the release of endorphins to the diencephalon and encaphalins to the cortical and subcortical regions of the brain. Panksepp (1998) proposes that both of these neuropeptides are released in response to positive attachment relationships.

Negative and traumatic situations lead to the release of stress hormones, which then prevents dopamine and endorphin activation, both of which are required for homeostasis and activation of reward and pleasure responses, positive social interactions, and stress management. Stress is a hyper-arousal response based in the hypothalamus, and release of stress hormones enables the self to take action to manage the stressful situation. If left in a hyper-aroused state for prolonged periods, stress can lead to individuals experiencing difficulty in regulating their own states and getting caught in negative behavioural and emotional loops, unable to adequately resource themselves. The role of the mother in the early life of an infant is to act as regulator for stress responses. All infants will experience stress, and it is the ability of the mother to respond to the child through interactive processes that enables the child to move through states of stress back to homeostasis. It is this process of asynchrony and synchrony with the mother that enables the infant later to self-correct and regulate affect (Schore, 2003a).

In infants who are handled well, cortisol receptors within the hippocampus are active and they are able to manage stressful situations as they have a secure base to return to. Where infants are handled less well and are left in stressful situations, this can be devastating to the developing brain resulting in memory difficulties and atrophy of cells within the hippocampus, which may lead to flat affect and lack of emotional response in stressful and relational situations.

Brief therapy and unconscious trauma

Where clients have experienced stress in their early lives that has led to developmental problems, such as attachment disorder, there is a greater need for right brain to right brain attunement within the therapy. Schore (2003b) proposes that where stressful memories are held deep within the unconscious, these may become activated wherever the self meets the other; that is, within the therapy process, particularly if the therapist focuses on a hopeful or positive future. Any right brain to right brain attunement risks activating unconscious stress reactions and, where this is an early unmet need, projective identification occurs (Schore, 2003a, p. 75). The therapist becomes the other, as the dysregulated self projects the intolerable aspects of themselves into the therapist. The client will then dissociate and become hypoactive. The role of the therapist in this situation is to respond to the dysregulated state in the client and find some way within the therapy to provide regulation for the ruptured self.

In some early stress responses and resultant damage, the unconscious memories are held in a dissociated format and are, therefore, disconnected from the higher cognitive structures, including the linguistic processing areas and the coherent meaning areas of the orbitofrontal cortex. Van der Kolk (2006) presents this as a challenge to the cognitive therapies that rely on understanding and insight.

He references Damasio when he suggests that "the rational, executive brain, the mind, the part that needs to be functional in order to engage in the process of psychotherapy, has very limited capacity to squelch sensations, control emotional arousal, or change fixed action patterns" (p. 5). It is only by working with the more somatic or unconscious aspects of the self through right brain processing, that regulation can occur. Therapies such as Ericksonian therapy, NLPt, and self relations therapy all provide the opportunity for this to occur, as do many of the body based therapies, such as drama therapy and Pesso–Boyden therapy.

This has considerable implications for the outcome-orientated nature of some therapies. Schore (2003a) quotes Freud on his view of this phenomena,

> "When one speaks hopefully to them or expresses satisfaction with the progress of treatment, they show signs of discontent and their condition invariably becomes worse" (Freud, 1923/1961b, p. 39). I suggest that in actuality this represents the therapist's misattunement to the patient's current state. [p. 28]

Therapies that offer validation and respect for the current presenting map, such as CAT, Ericksonian therapy, NLPt, self relations therapy, and SFBT provide greater potential for preventing misattunement. O'Hanlon and Bertolino (1998) and O'Hanlon (2003) has further developed the theme of validation within SFBT in his possibility and inclusive therapy. His inclusive therapy provides the potential for inclusion of seeming opposites; for example, it is all right to feel like ending your life and it is all right to go on living as well.

Theoretical principles of goal activation

The neuroscience theory

Arousal responses within the subcortical structures are based within the reticular activation system, the control centre of the brain responsible for self-regulation, balance, and harmony within the nervous system, and activation of the arousal towards motivational states (Solms, 1996). This system is responsible for focus of attention and flexibility of orientation, that is, what we pay attention to

at a conscious level, what we see, how we respond to these observations, and how we then act in response to our observations.
Sensory stimuli pass through the reticular activation system, both
internally derived and externally observed. This system is
discussed in depth by Hart (2008, Chapter Six). As the reticular activation system is accessed during goal activation, neuropeptides are
released that then result in an increase in blood flow and oxygen to
the area of the body responsible for behaviours that will lead to
actualization of the goal.

Social development theory

Within social development theory, there are three theories that are
considered to be important in the development of behavioural traits
that lead towards goal activation and associated behavioural
response. These are classical conditioning, operant conditioning,
and social learning theory.

Classic conditioning (Pavlov, 1927) demonstrates that reflex
behaviours occur in response to specific stimuli, which can be positive and negative. In his experiments, physiologist Pavlov demonstrated that dogs have a salivary reflex that could be conditioned to
unnatural stimuli, such as ringing a buzzer, and that where this
stimulus is linked to the dog's food, the dog would develop an
associated response between the stimuli of the buzzer and food,
even when the food was not shown. He was also able to demonstrate how conditioned responses could also be eliminated, using a
similar process. Watson and Reyner (1920) further developed this
work, and demonstrated that fear in infants could be conditioned
and eliminated using the same principles. These conditioned
responses then become generalized over time, and as we grow, we
continue patterns of association between stimuli that result in positive feelings and repeating these, and avoiding stimuli that result in
negative feelings. Adler (1992) and Pert (1997) both added to this
theory and included the theory of state dependent recall, which
proposes that a person is more likely to recall positive emotional
experiences when in a good state and negative emotional experiences when in a bad state. Damasio (1994) identified that conditioning involves excitation of neurons which hold a neural memory in
response to the impulse, resulting in the release of neurotransmitters

and activation of the next neuron, and, hence, activation of the entire neurological chain, leading to a behavioural response.

Operant conditioning (Skinner, 1938) is based on Thorndike's (1913) Law of Effect, which states that behaviour resulting in pleasant consequences is more likely to be repeated, whereas behaviour that does not result in such an effect tends to die away. Skinner proposed that individuals will generalize on behavioural responses in situations which are similar to the original one where the conditioned response was developed. He developed his theory further to include negative reinforcement, or escape learning, where we remove or avoid something unpleasant.

Social learning theory emerged from both classical and operant conditioning, with Bandura (1977) proposing that children learn from observing others and are more likely to imitate a behaviour if the model is similar in some way to themselves, demonstrates power or control over some desirable object, is seen to be rewarded for their actions, and are warm and nurturing. Bandura also focused on the more cognitive elements of learning as being key elements of social learning theory: paying attention to certain aspects of the model while ignoring irrelevant or distracting aspects; retaining accurate features of the model in memory; able to accurately duplicate the model's behaviour; and being motivated to reproduce the behaviour justified by perceived rewards.

Attachment theory

Within the attachment process, the reticular activation system can develop fully through care-giver interaction or can be damaged, resulting in lack of activity and concentration.

Stern (1998) suggests that infant behaviour is already goal orientated by the age of 3–4 months. Stern refers to "instrumental crying" (p. 92), where an infant utilizes goal-orientated behaviours for specific tasks towards the object. This then develops into a goal-corrected partnership with the care-giver by the time the child is of pre-school age. The healthy child is able to balance his attachment-related goals with those of the desire to explore. Bowlby (1969) proposes that goal-corrected behaviour only occurs when the child is able to balance his own needs with those of the maternal figure.

Richardson (in Sinason, 2002, p. 152) proposes that infants who have developed a dissociated self, as a result of trauma, experience disorganized goal-seeking behaviour. They maintain a goal towards the care-giver as the only possible source of refuge, and yet have developed conflicting goal-directed behaviours that serve to maintain a safe distance from the untrustworthy care-giver and to separate away from the fragmented and traumatized aspects of the self.

Schore's research has demonstrated the crucial role that the orbital prefrontal region has in regulating emotional and motivational states (2003a, pp. 255–256), and that it is this area of the brain that is key to affect regulation in attachment relationships.

Brief therapy theories

Each of the brief therapies assumes an outcome for therapy that is goal orientated for the client. By accepting the notion of a goal that can be achieved, a presupposition occurs that a solution exists for the problem state and that it can be achieved. This immediately stimulates the reticular activation system (RAS), which is responsible for self-regulation and organized mental activity. By adding visualization processes to the cognitive components of goal setting, the full potential of the RAS, through increased arousal and attention responses, is harnessed, and the client's nervous system is stimulated towards goal-seeking behaviour.

Erickson suggests that the goals of pursuit of meaningful labour, a vigilant readiness to avoid harm and to live a long life provide direction and meaning, and it is only by focusing on these that an integrated sense of self can emerge (Short, Erickson, & Erickson Klein, 2005, p. 17). This often occurs through a series of small steps, rather than setting the client a goal that seems to be unattainable and may add to any current fear of failure. As these small steps are achieved, the client sets up generalized patterns of response, and these become normal ways of functioning, making it easier to move towards longer term and bigger goals. Incremental here and now successes can be built on to facilitate the client to a longer-term strategic change (*ibid.*, pp. 82–83).

Within SFBT, goals are defined as a presence of solutions rather than an absence of problems. Similar to Ericksonian approaches, they are realistic and achievable for the individual and are described in interactional and social contexts. They also need to be important enough for the client to achieve, and involve an element of hard work to enable achievement.

Patterns of motivation

Hart (2008) identifies two systems of motivation in the brain, the pleasure and reward system, and the fear and anxiety system.

In the pleasure and reward system, the dopamine circuit is activated in response to pleasurable stimuli and positive rewards. Within the process of pleasure and reward there are primary and secondary inducers. Primary inducers are direct pleasurable responses, such as food, nurture, warmth, and sexual stimuli, whereas secondary inducers occur as conditioned responses to specific stimuli. These are known as goal orientated, or towards based values or motivational traits. Panksepp (1998) proposes that these are at two levels, goal-orientated behaviour that is directly linked to our survival, such as food, warmth, and sex, and goal-orientated behaviour that is directly linked to cognitive meaning.

The fear and anxiety systems are also motivational responses, with fear being an externally driven motivation and anxiety an internally driven motivation. Separation anxiety is a fear-driven response, and is directly linked to the attachment system. Primary and secondary inducers are also present within the fear and anxiety systems, with primary inducers being direct responses to fearful situations and secondary inducers being associated and conditioned responses, for example, hearing an ambulance siren and immediately associating to a previous situation of being taken to hospital in an ambulance.

Within these two systems there is a strong correlation to Freud's concept of the pleasure/pain principle: that we will move towards and relate more strongly to situations that bring pleasure and we will move away from and avoid situations that bring us pain or discomfort.

Cognitive analytic therapy recognizes both pleasure–reward and fear–anxiety motivational responses, and sees these as being roles that individuals play in response to behavioural stimuli from others. The purpose of CAT is to facilitate the client to change their pattern of behaviour and move towards more useful responses. This can be directly linked to the classic and operant conditioning theories, where the client learns to un-condition their responses.

Cognitive behavioural therapy, although initially developed to work with conditioned responses and social learning theory, focuses now on enabling the client to gain greater understanding of the relationship between thoughts, feelings, and behaviour. The client is actively discouraged from making links to past problems and experiences, potentially limiting the amount of change that can be done using operant conditioning theory. The approach focuses on trying out new ways of behaving, which has the potential of developing new neural networks, as suggested by Goleman (2003) and LeDoux (2001). CBT also considers the fear–anxiety system, and works with clients to enable them to face their fears, testing these out to disprove them.

Eye movement desensitization and reprocessing focuses specifically on the neurological elements of negative emotional states and, thereby, the negative neurological pathways that have created the state. It works by releasing traumatic and negative memories that are held within the neural networks. It utilizes the principles of creating new conditioned neurological responses as new memories and associations are created (Damasio, 1994). Shapiro has demonstrated that memories are held as incomplete within the fear and anxiety system, and that by connecting the client to more resourceful ways of responding found in other neurological networks, the client can literally collapse the old association. By working with visualization processes, EMDR directly accesses the reticular activation system, enabling the linking of memory components. A collapsing of conditioned responses also occurs through the repeated accessing and dismissal of traumatic imagery, resulting in the desensitization process identified by Skinner (1938).

Ericksonian therapy recognizes the pleasure and reward system and views all symptoms as being desirous of growth and change. Ericksonian therapy utilizes representations of the fear and anxiety system by breaking these components of problem states into smaller and more manageable chunks, enabling partitioning of the unconscious neurological components. By reducing the fear and anxiety response, the client then develops a perception that the problem is changing and gains an alternative perspective towards a more pleasurable and reward-related response. This model of therapy also allows for validation and acceptance of the more shameful aspects of the self that are held within the anxiety system, thereby reducing the negative impact that these can have, as the client no longer needs to work actively to repress them.

Neurolinguistic psychotherapy recognizes and utilizes classical and operant conditioning, social learning theory, and motivational patterns of both pleasure–reward and anxiety–fear. In classic and operant conditioning, a process has been developed, anchoring, that utilizes triggered responses to create more useful states and motivation around specific context areas. The process also enables the collapsing of negative triggered responses. NLPt is focused on goal orientation, and all processes are specifically designed to activate the reward–pleasure motivation patterns. NLPt also includes enabling the client to understand their own motivational patterns through values. This process enables the client to recognize, understand, and alter self-limiting patterns of behaviour (Wake, 2008).

Provocative therapy directly utilizes the fear–anxiety system of the client to access the pleasure–reward system. The client's self-limiting patterns of behaviour are lampooned, with the therapist working with the client in accessing the reticular activation system through positive and spontaneous imagery.

Rational emotive behaviour therapy is predominantly focused on accessing the pleasure–reward motivations, operating from a view that the primary goal in life is to stay alive and pursue happiness. The focus of REBT is to enable the client to become aware of what prevents them achieving happiness and to assist them in overcoming these blocks; that is, to remove the fear and anxiety responses.

Self relations therapy also focuses on accessing the pleasurable–reward motivations to achieve happiness and health, and utilizing the fear–anxiety responses to enable helpfulness and healing of self and others. The two motivational systems are viewed as dynamic processes that we will access cyclically throughout our life, and it is only by accessing, acknowledging, and responding to our fear–anxiety responses that we can then move to responses of pleasure and reward. Self relations therapy enables the movement through fear and anxiety responses, rather than adopting a flight/freeze response. By doing this, we can gain connection through suffering, rather than becoming overwhelmed by it.

Solution focused brief therapy utilizes only the pleasure–reward system and immediately reframes to find exceptions when the fear–anxiety system is activated. SFBT assumes that the client's system holds a capacity for finding a more desirable way of being. Similar to Ericksonian therapy, the model utilizes small steps of change that lead to generalized patterns of response and a pruning away of the fear–anxiety response. SFBT helps people to see what they want in visual, behavioural terms. The preferred future is a pointer to doing something different in the future, which can result in prompting the reticular activation system to facilitate goal achievement.

Goal-setting processes

There are many examples of goal-setting processes that are present in the brief therapies, some of which are more comprehensive than others. Others are quite simplistic, using processes such as SMART (specific, measurable, achievable, realistic, and timed) steps to enable achievement of the goal.

I have included here two examples of comprehensive goal-setting processes, one from NLPt (Table 5) and the other from SFBT (see Table 6).

Goal setting and utilization process within SFBT

SFBT is outcome-orientated throughout. After exploring the client's preferred future, the therapist then moves the client to the scale to look at what they have done to get to where they are.

Summarized in Table 6 are types of goal-orientated questions that can be used within the first (and subsequent) sessions of SFBT.

Accessing, setting up, and utilizing triggered responses

Classical and operant conditioning can be utilized as processes within the therapy session. They can be used consciously and unconsciously, and are an effective way of enabling the client to reduce or negate old patterns of behaviour. This process is referred

Table 5.   Well formed outcome process of NLPt.

Step	Question	Comments
1. Positive	What do you want? What will this bring you?	It is important that the client states what they want and not what they don't want. If the client presents a negative, then ask the question, "What do you want instead?" Sometimes clients will want a goal that is low level and may only be environmental, e.g., "I want to get some sleep." By asking the question, "What will this bring you?", the client is required to chunk up and expand their focus to the benefits, e.g. more energy and peace of mind. Sleep can be achieved through medication; more energy and peace of mind activates the pleasure–reward system.
2. Achievement	How will you know when you are succeeding? How will you know when you have got it? What will you see, hear and feel? How will someone else know when you have got it?	Activates the neural pathway of evidence base for the goal. By visualizing evidence of achievement of the goal, it is as if it has already happened, and the client will develop an internal image of achievement of the goal. Activating the RAS and particularly the visual component. This encourages the client to dissociate from achievement of the goal and enhances the motivation towards the achievement of it.

(continued)

Table 5.   Well formed outcome process of NLPt.

Step	Question	Comments
		By remaining dissociated from something that we want, the more desirable it becomes. Think about a favourite food; imagine it in front of you, still in its wrapper, or on the plate. Now imagine the empty wrapper or plate. Which is more desirable?
	What is the first step?	Begins to activate the neural pathways and behaviours that are directly responsible for achievement of the goal. Links the neurological path way through to direct attainment of the goal, from first to last step.
	What is the last step?	
3. Context	When, where, and with whom do you want it?	There may be some situations where the goal is inappropriate and may result in activation of the fear–anxiety response. For example, if the client wants to be sexually confident, this will work for them in their immediate relationship; however, it may not be appropriate for them to act in this way with their Board of Directors.
	When, where and with whom do you not want it? How long for?	The client may wish to be confident in applying for a new job and develop self belief such that they can attain promotion, and they may also find it helpful to be clear about the limitations that they may apply to the kind of jobs that they may consider.

(continued)

Table 5.   (*continued*)

Step	Question	Comments
4. Ecology	What time will this outcome need? Who else is affected and how will they feel? How does it fit in with your other outcomes? How does it increase your choices?	The client will want to consider how achieving the outcome will affect the wider system. It may have an impact on resources such as finance and time. It may have an impact on other people, on other roles they play in their life and on the choices it gives them.
	What will happen if you get it? What won't happen if you get it? What will happen if you don't get it? What won't happen if you don't get it?	These four questions are based in quantum linguistics (Chen, 2002) and will facilitate the freeing of linguistic double binds if they are asked of the client (Wake, 2008, pp. 98–101).
5. Resources	Can you start and maintain it? What resources have you already got? (Skills, people, money, objects etc.) What resources do you need?	This condition is about how much direct control the person setting it has over the achievement of the outcome and how much other people will be involved. There is little point in the client working on goals that they have little direct control over.
	Who has already succeeded in achieving this outcome?	This enables utilization of social learning theory, by encouraging modelling of a successful other.

to as anchoring. Anchoring is one of the most simple and powerful tools for being able to select and access internal states. Each state will be associated with the total context in which it occurred, both the internal and external conditions, what the client was doing,

Table 6.   Goal-orientated questions for use in SFBT.

Step	Question	Comments
Problem free talk	"I know very little about you apart from what brings you here. What would you feel happy to tell me about yourself?" "What are you interested in?" "What do you enjoy?" "What are you good at?" "What about family?" "How would your best friend describe you?"	Assumes pleasure–reward motivation from the beginning.
Pre-treatment change	"Often between making an appointment and arriving for that appointment, people have already noticed a change. What have you noticed?"	Presupposing that change has already occurred and bringing this to the client's attention.
Best hopes for the session	"What are your best hopes for this session?" "How will you know that it was useful coming here today?" "What will it take for you to say that this has been worthwhile?"	Presupposing and enabling a future orientation for the session. Also presupposes what difference the session will lead to.
Preferred future	"Imagine that after you have gone to bed tonight a miracle happens and the problem that brought you here today is resolved. But since you are asleep you will not know that the miracle has happened. When you wake up tomorrow morning, what will be different that will tell you? What will you see yourself doing differently, what will you see others doing differently that will tell you that the miracle has happened?"	This utilizes activation of the reticular activation system and visualization towards an assumed positive future, immediately developing a pleasure–reward response in the client. (There are further questions within the preferred future that enable the therapist to focus the client on more specific aspects of the preferred future, depending on presentation.)

(continued)

Table 6. (*continued*)

Step	Question	Comments
Exceptions	"When are the times that it doesn't happen?" "When are the times that it doesn't last long?" "When are the times that it seems to be less intense?" "When are the times that you feel better?" "When are the times that it bothers you least?" "When do you resist the urge to . . .?"	Moving the client from fear–anxiety system to times when it is not activated, enabling the the development of more generalized times when the problem state does not exist.
Coping	"So what has been helping you to survive?" "How have you been getting through?" "How come you have not given up hope?" "So how come you managed to get here today?" "What do you think your best friend, for example, most admires about the way that you have been struggling with this?" "How do you cope?" "That situation sounds pretty overwhelming: how do you get by?" "What is it that even gives you the strength to get up in the morning?"	This process accesses elements of resiliency and motivation within the client, even when the odds are against them. This activates greater potential within the goal-seeking behaviour.
Scales	"On a scale of 0–10, with 0 being the worst that things have been in your life and 10 representing how you want things to be, where are you today?"	By breaking down the components into a scaling system, it is possible to start to compartmentalize the problem state and generalize on the motivational factors that will move the client towards solution state.

(*continued*)

Table 6.   (*continued*)

Step	Question	Comments
	"So what is it that you are doing that means that you are at . . . and not at 0?" "So, if you are on 3, tell me what you will be doing that will tell you that you are on 4?"	
Locating resources and building on strengths	"When you faced this sort of problem in the past, how did you resolve it?" "How would you know that you were doing that again?" "What other tough situations have you handled?" "What did handling that that well tell you about yourself?"	Accessing resourceful neurological connections when faced with previous situations triggering the fear–anxiety system.

what they were feeling, and what they were thinking. An anchor includes the sensory input, visual (image), auditory (sound), kinaesthetic (feeling or sensation), olfactory (smell), or gustatory (taste) that was part of the original experience. It can also be a word or the label that has been given to the state.

Anchors always involve a stimulus and a response. In using anchors with a client, there are a number of processes that can be utilized to enable the client to have greater choice in managing their state: resource anchor; collapsing negative anchors; chaining anchors.

There are a number of keys that enable anchors to be utilized effectively.

● The more intense a remembered experience and state, the easier it is to anchor, with the anchor/stimulus applied at the peak of the experience.

- Timing is essential; the stimulus is applied just before the state reaches its peak and removed as soon as it has reached the peak.
- Uniqueness of the stimulus will enable the client to ensure that the state is only accessed when they want it to be accessed, rather than be triggered unintentionally (e.g., a handshake could be triggered unintentionally).
- Replication of the stimulus will maintain and increase its power. Pavlov demonstrated that the stimulus response lessened over time the more it was used, therefore it is important to reset the anchor.
- Additionally, the more times the anchor is applied, the more powerful it will be (Figure 3).

Applying the anchor

See Table 7.

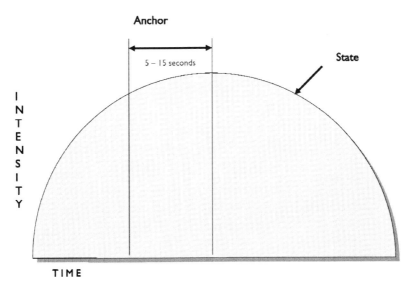

Figure 3.   The process of anchoring.

Table 7.   Applying an anchor.

Process	Dialogue
1. Rapport	
2. Set outcome with the client and decide on the state that will have the largest impact on resourcing them for the outcome.	
3. Set the frame and ask permission to touch the client.	In a moment we're going to do some anchoring which uses stimulus response to integrate some new neurological choices for you. Where do you want to physically anchor this new state? Is it all right to touch you there?
4. Recall Get yourself into the state you are eliciting. Make sure the client is in a fully associated, intense, congruent state.	Can you remember a time when you were totally (*state*)? Can you remember a specific time? As you go back to that time now (pause), go right back to that time, float down into your body and see what you see, hear what you hear, and really feel the feelings of being totally (*state*), as if now.
5. Anchor Anchor the state by touching the client when the experience has become the strongest. (Alternatively, you may want to help the client set the anchor for himself or herself). Intensify that state by holding the anchor down through the peak of the experience.	
6. Break state Use a pattern interrupt and repeat steps 4, 5, and 6 as necessary. (3 or 4 times.)	
7. Test Fire the anchor and watch the response.	

Collapsing anchors

Collapsing anchors is a useful technique to use when a client habit-ually responds in an unresourceful way to a particular situation, and enables the client to link more positive states to the situation. It is particularly useful when the client is operating an "away from" motivation pattern and wishes to change it to a "towards" motiva-tion response, for example, moving from a fear response to an accepting, happy, or calm response. The process is similar to that of setting a resource anchor with an added component of collapsing the negative state into the positive one (Table 8).

Chaining anchors

Chaining anchors is a technique that can be used when the gap between the present state and the desired state is large. The process works by using a series of intermediate states to move the person's neurology from the present state to the desired state in small steps rather than one leap (Figure 4).

In designing the chain, the first intermediate state is an "away from" state that will move the client out of their present state. The next intermediate state is a "towards" state that will take them towards their end state. It is also important that the states are not similar to the current strategy that the client is using (Table 9).

Utilizing associated and dissociated states

As clients recall experiences in their lives, they may recall these as associated or dissociated memories. When a client is recalling an experience and views it through his own eyes, as if it were occur-ring now, he is experiencing the event in an associated form. Clients who can recall events and view the event as if they are watching a film, or picture, of themselves are experiencing the event in a disso-ciated form. By enabling a client to gain greater flexibility in moving between associated and dissociated states, the client will be able to make the most appropriate choice for herself with regard to how she feels about events.

Clients who experience all events in an associated form will feel good in any positive experience and will also feel negative in less

Table 8.   The process leading to the collapsing of anchors.

Process	Dialogue
1. Rapport	
2. Set outcome with the client and decide on the state that will have the largest impact on resourcing them for the outcome and identify the negative state to be collapsed.	
3. Set the frame and ask permission to touch the client	In a moment we're going to do some anchoring, which uses stimulus response to integrate some new neurological choices for you. Where do you want to physically anchor these states? Is it all right to touch you there?
4. Recall Get yourself into the state you are eliciting. Make sure the client is in a fully associated, intense, congruent state.	Can you remember a time when you were totally (*state*)? Can you remember a specific time? As you go back to that time now (pause), go right back to that time, float down into your body and see what you see, hear what you hear, and really feel the feelings of being totally (*state*), as if now.
5. Anchor the positive state Anchor the state by touching the client when the experience has become the strongest. Intensify that state by holding the anchor down through the peak of the experience. Stack this state by reapplying the anchor several times.	
6. Break state Use a pattern interrupt.	
7. Anchor the negative state Ask the person to recall the negative state, and you anchor it in a different place. You anchor it only once, and so you have a weak negative anchor and elsewhere you have set a strong and powerful positive anchor.	Can you remember a time when you were totally (*negative state*)? Can you remember a specific time? As you go back to that time now (pause), go right back to that time, float down into your body and see what you see, hear what you hear, and really feel the feelings of being totally (*state*), as if now.

(*continued*)

Table 8.   (continued)

Process	Dialogue
8. Fire both anchors at the same time Watch carefully as the states integrate. Once you notice that the person is steady and integrated, then remove the negative anchor and hold on the positive one for a further five seconds and then release it.	
7. Test Future pace by asking them to thinkabout a time in the future when the old state may have arisen. How do they now feel about it?	

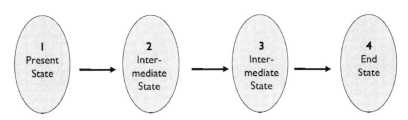

Figure 4.   Chaining anchors: a process used to move a person from the present state to the desired state in small steps.

pleasant experiences. They may feel themselves becoming over-whelmed with emotions at times, and may find it difficult to gain an objective perspective on events.

Clients who experience all events in a dissociated form will find it easier to handle more difficult situations, and this would also mean that they are not as engaged in positive experiences.

Some clients may find that they are associated into negative experiences and remain dissociated from positive experiences. This can often happen in clients who experience depression, where they have lost joy, meaning, and hope in their lives. Other clients may associate into the positive experiences and remain dissociated from the negative. This enables them to distance themselves from nega-tive experiences and fully enjoy positive experiences.

Table 9. Designing the chain of anchors.

Process	Dialogue
1. Rapport	
2. *Set outcome* with the client and decide on the unresourceful state to be collapsed.	
3. *Identify the desired end state* What state would you like instead?	
4. Set the frame *and ask permission to touch the client*	In a moment we're going to do some anchoring, which uses stimulus response to integrate some new neurological choices for you. Where do you want to physically anchor these states? Is it all right to touch you there?
5. *Design the chain.* Identify each of the intermediate states and decide on the order.	
6. *Elicit and anchor each state separately.*	
7. *Test each anchor.* Break state between each anchor test.	
8. *Chain the states by:*	
Fire Anchor 1	[1] [2] [3] [4]
At its peak, also fire Anchor 2	↓ [1] [2] [3] [4]
Release 1	
When 2 is at its peak, also fire anchor 3	[1] [2] [3] [4]
Release 2	↓ [1] [2] [3] [4]
When 3 is at its peak, also fire anchor 4	[1] [2] [3] [4]
Release 3	↓ [1] [2] [3] [4]
Watch anchor 4 peak	[1] [2] [3] [4]
9. *Test—fire present state Anchor 1* The client should end up in the desired end state.	↓ [1] [2] [3] [4]

Clients can be supported to develop greater association into experiences through anchoring, described earlier in the chapter, and also through visualization. By asking a client to make an internal picture of his experience and then asking him to change the picture so that he is looking through his own eyes, you can assist him to associate into experiences. Equally, by asking the client to make a picture of an associated experience that he wants to feel less involved with, and then asking him to change the picture so that he can see himself in it can assist dissociation. Further details of submodality processes are available in the writings of Andreas and Andreas (1987).

In goal setting, future desired states are always dissociated, which enables maintenance of motivation towards the goal. It is far more compelling to imagine something exciting happening in the future than it is to imagine it having already happened or be in the process of it happening.

CHAPTER SIX

The therapist's role in brief therapy

The therapist's role in regulating affective states

Gerhardt (2004) proposes that, in early development, we learn to modulate our own states by monitoring the states of others to ensure that we can maintain the relationship that is essential for our survival. This is done through observing visual cues, such as facial expression, which leads to attachment and social learning. When we observe someone else's behaviour, the same neurons become activated in our own neurology. Gerhardt (*ibid.*) refers to Davidson and Fox's work (1982) when she says that "babies who see happy behaviour have activated left frontal brains and babies who witness sad behaviour have activated right frontal brains" (p. 31).

Schore provides a more comprehensive description of this process, stating that

> only in a right hemispheric-dominant receptive state in which a "private self" is communicating with another "private self" can a self–self object system of spontaneous affective transference–countertransference communications be developed. [2003a, p. 51]

He continues to comment that

> a state of resonance exists when the therapist's subjectivity is
> empathically attuned to the patient's inner state (one that may be
> unconscious to the patient), and this *resonance* then interactively
> amplifies, in both intensity and duration, the affective state *in both*
> *members of the dyad* [*ibid.*]

Schore highlights this, as the "coconstructed intersubjective field of
the patient and therapist are temporarily coactivated and coupled,
deactivated and uncoupled, or reactivated and recoupled". This
directly resonates with the descriptions of the therapeutic work of
Gilligan's self relations therapy, Gawler-Wright's NLPt, and Ericksonian therapy. The therapist acts as regulator for the client's affective state.

Schore (2003a, pp. 279–281) lists the principles of psychotherapeutic treatment of early-forming, right-hemispheric self pathologies. I have summarized these (a comprehensive list is available
within the appendices of *Affect Regulation and Repair of the Self*,
2003a), and mapped them against the known processes within the
brief therapies (Table 10).

Rapport in therapy

Both Schore and Gerhardt are referring to processes within the
brain that Glaser and colleagues have identified as the mirror
neuron system (Glaser, Grezes, Calvo, Passingham, & Haggard,
2004). They found that when we observe an image of an individual
moving, the pre-motor cortex is stimulated and the brain resonates
to the image being shown. Their study also demonstrated that
familiarity and emotion engagement systems are also influenced by
motor repertoire. It is this right brain to right brain process that is
stimulated in rapport.

Erickson believed that rapport was fundamental to his therapy
being successful. He considered that therapy "involves constant
realignment of the direction of therapy to match the patient's meanings and preferences (Duncan, Miller and Sparks, 2004, p. 192)" (in
Short, Erickson, & Erickson Klein, 2005, p. 29). When the therapist
is in rapport with the client's unconscious mind, they are directly

Table 10.   Summary of the principles of psychotherapeutic treatment of self pathologies (Schore, 2003a).

Schore's principle	Presence within the brief therapies
1. Conceptualization of self psychopathology as deficits of affect regulation—formulation of a treatment model matched to developmental level	CAT Ericksonian therapy NLPt Self relations therapy
2. Model of right brain interactive affect regulation as fundamental process of psychobiological development and psychotherapeutic treatment	CAT EMDR Ericksonian therapy NLPt Provocative therapy REBT Self relations therapy
3. Focus on identification and integration of non-conscious biological states of mind–body	CAT EMDR Ericksonian therapy NLPt REBT Self relations therapy SFBT
4. Understanding of therapeutic empathy, right brain, non-verbal psychobiological attunement. Use of affect synchronizing transactions that forge the patient's attachment to the therapist.	CAT Ericksonian therapy REBT Self relations therapy
5. Operational definition of therapeutic alliance in terms of non-conscious, yet mutually reciprocal influences. The patient's capacity for attachment combines with the therapist's contingently-responsive facilitating behaviours.	CAT Ericksonian therapy REBT Self relations therapy SFBT
6. Therapist is experienced as being in a state of vitalizing attunement to the patient, resonating with the patient's right brain.	CAT Ericksonian therapy Self relations therapy
7. Stress on dysregulated right brain "primitive affects" and identification of unconscious dissociated affects that were never developmentally interactively regulated, rather than analysis of unconscious resistance and disavowal of repressed affect	CAT EMDR Ericksonian therapy NLPt Provocative therapy REBT Self relations therapy

(continued)

Table 10. (*continued*)

Schore's principle	Presence within the brief therapies
8. Awareness of clinician's right hemispheric, countertransferential visceral–somatic responses to the patient's transferential affects. Attention to the intensity, duration, frequency and lability of the patient's internal state.	CAT Self relations therapy
9. Moment-to-moment tracking of content-associated subtle and dramatic shifts in arousal and state in patient narratives Identification of non-conscious "hot" cognitions that dysregulate self function.	CAT CBT Ericksonian therapy NLPt Provocative therapy REBT Self relations therapy SFBT
10. Awareness of dyadically triggered non-verbal shame dynamics, and co-creation of interpersonal context within the therapeutic alliance that allows for deeper self revelation.	CAT Ericksonian therapy Self relations therapy
11. Conception of defence mechanisms as non-conscious strategies of emotional regulation for avoiding, minimizing, or converting affects that are intolerable. Emphasis on dissociation and projective identification as ways of defending against intense affects that can disorganize the self system	Ericksonian therapy Self relations therapy
12. Uncovering of insecure attachment histories imprinted and stored as right hemispheric working models.	CAT REBT Self relations therapy
13. Identification of early-forming,rapid-acting, and non-conscious right brain perceptual biases for detecting threatening social stimuli. Enactments occur as stress coping strategies.	CAT CBT EMDR Ericksonian therapy NLPt Provocative therapy REBT Self relations therapy SFBT
14. Appreciation of the centrality of interactive repair as a therapeutic mechanism—facilitates mutual regulation of affective homeostasis.	CAT Ericksonian therapy Self relations therapy (*continued*)

Table 10.   (continued)

Schore's principle	Presence within the brief therapies
15. Understanding that the therapist's affect tolerance is a critical factor determining the range, types, and intensities of emotions that are explored or disavowed in the therapy.	
16. Emphasis on the process rather than genetic interpretations. Attention to right hemisphere emotion communicating as well as linguistic content of interpretations.	EMDR Ericksonian therapy NLPt Provocative therapy REBT Self relations therapy SFBT
17. Directing of therapeutic technique towards the elevation of emotions from a primitive form to a mature symbolic representation level. Creation of self reflective position that can appraise significance and meaning of affects.	CAT CBT Ericksonian therapy NLPt Provocative therapy REBT Self relations therapy SFBT
18. Growth facilitating therapeutic environment that enables a modulated self system that can integrate a broad range of affects	CAT Ericksonian therapy NLPt REBT Self relations therapy SFBT
19. Restoration and expansion of patient's capacity for self-regulation. Flexibly regulate emotional states in interactions with others. Autonomous autoregulation and resilience to shift between these two modes.	CAT Ericksonian therapy NLPt Provocative therapy REBT SFBT
20. Long term goal of reorganizing insecure internal working models into earned secure models. Development of the ability to maintain a coherent, continuous and unified sense of self.	CAT Ericksonian therapy NLPt Provocative therapy REBT Self relations therapy SFBT

linking to the right brain to right brain attunement process that Schore (2003a) refers to.

Rapport, as a process of responsiveness, includes a number of elements. Merhabian (1981) highlighted the relative importance of words *vs.* non-verbal cues. His study dealt with all facets of non-verbal communication, including body posture and movements, facial expressions, voice quality and intonation during speech, volume and speed of speech, and subtle variations in wording of sentences. His findings proposed that for total liking (and responsiveness), 7% was verbal liking, 38% was vocal liking, and 55% was facial liking. It is possible, therefore, for the therapist to utilize these aspects by matching or mirroring them when developing the therapeutic relationship with the client.

When this process of utilizing rapport is linked to other therapeutic skills, such as utilization of sensory-based language, accessing of the visual, auditory, and kinaesthetic systems, and the use of indirect suggestion, sensory stimuli travel through the brain using multiple pathways, thereby creating multiple implicit memories (Short, Erickson, & Erickson Klein, 2005, p. 125).

Therapy for therapists?

In considering this process within Schore's work, it is essential that therapists are also aware of, and can regulate, their own affective states. Of the modalities reviewed in this book, very few of them require the therapist to be in therapy for the duration of their training and, for some therapies, there is no requirement for any form of personal therapy. This raises questions concerning the ability of therapists to be able to respond to the therapeutic principles outlined by Schore (2003a). The following elements pertinent to the role of the therapist are outlined by Schore as being critical to psychotherapeutic treatment:

- right brain interactive processes that affect regulation;
- therapeutic empathy and right brain non-verbal psychobiological attunement;
- affect synchronizing transactions that enable development of attachment to the therapist;

- patient attachment with the therapist having contingently responsive facilitating behaviours;
- therapist vitalizing attunement to the patient's right brain;
- the therapist being aware of right hemispheric countertransferential visceral–somatic responses;
- cocreation of interpersonal context that allows for deeper self revelation;
- containing and utilizing dissociation and projective identification processes;
- interactive repair as a therapeutic mechanism;
- understanding of the therapist's affect tolerance;

Each of these points requires the therapist to have a high level of self-awareness and a comprehensive awareness and understanding of their own affective states, both conscious and non-conscious. A question that has been debated within the brief therapy world is the requirement for prolonged periods of personal therapy for the therapist during their training. Some of the above processes can be developed and attuned within the therapist through processes other than personal therapy. Mindfulness training, reflective practice, peer support groups, and self-exploration workshops are some of the possible alternatives to personal therapy; however, each of these would be required to demonstrate greater understanding and increase in the therapist's awareness and ability to tolerate high levels of affect.

Client case studies of affect regulation and repair

Each of these case studies is presented with the full permission of the individual. Studies have been anonymized, with some details changed to maintain client confidentiality. The studies provide examples of the brief therapeutic process, and highlight where affect regulation and repair have occurred within the therapy.

Julie

Julie was referred to me for therapy via her workplace. She had been experiencing a stressful time in her personal life and this was beginning to have an impact on her work. On presentation, Julie appeared stressed and was hyper manic in affect. She expressed feelings of being stressed out and not being in control. She was able to describe the main causes of stress: she had a young child, worked full-time, her marriage was in difficulty, and because of her busy schedule and requirement to travel with her work, she was finding it difficult to spend any time taking care of her own needs.

Her family upbringing had been chaotic, with occasional episodes of domestic violence that she witnessed. Her father had serial affairs and her mother coped with this by threatening to kill herself regularly, finally committing suicide when Julie was in her early thirties. Julie was an only child and felt responsible for her mother throughout her life, her mother using this as a way of controlling Julie, with both parents blaming her for things that were wrong in the marriage. After her mother's death, her father remarried, quickly, someone who was quite a bit younger than Julie. Julie found this difficult to accept, and now has an on/off relationship with her father.

In her adult personal relationships, Julie had created some repeating patterns of behaviour. She initially described all of her previous intimate relationships with men as being with individuals who were less successful than her, either financially, with less motivation, or intellectually. I asked her to describe each of the relationships in turn, and her perception of their inferiority to her was not mirrored in her description of each of the relationships. For many of these relationships, the individuals were usually financially successful; however, she found that there were often aspects of their behaviour that she could not control, either drinking too much, smoking, or having affairs. One individual was particularly successful and would treat her "like a princess". When I asked her about this and why the relationship had ended, she said that she didn't like being treated as someone special—"I feel as if I owe them something".

Julie's history appears to mirror that found in individuals with avoidant attachment structures. She worked very hard as a child to protect her parents from her feelings, for fear of making matters worse, and she also absorbed a lot of her mother's distress. This manifested in her adult life with no real sense of self in a relationship, and she would find it very difficult to be in a relationship where security and stability were available. She constantly felt not good enough, and would find it easier to maintain relationships as friendships long after the intimate relationship had ended.

My approach with Julie was to work with NLPt and to also use the psychodynamic process to create a sense of structure and positive attachment. The initial sessions focused on goal setting and starting her reticular activation system, so that she became more aware of what she did want in a relationship, rather than what she did not want. As the therapy continued and we started to address the underlying avoidant patterns, Julie became more dysfunctional, often finding it difficult to contain her feelings between sessions. We agreed a more open contract of therapy, and had telephone sessions in between her regular appointments. Over time, Julie was able to identify and access a strong sense of self that existed outside of relationships, and we were able to utilize this as a resource to begin to bring this into her current relationship. She began to work on two main areas: "Who am I in a relationship?", and "What does it mean if my partner wants to give me something in a relationship?" From this, she identified that she could only exist in a relationship if she kept herself distant and could access an adult ego state of superiority and arrogance. Trust became a central theme to the therapy, and we worked through the emotional and cognitive meanings that this had for her. I used elements of self-disclosure to mirror a trusting relationship with her. From this, she was then able to look at her own marriage in more depth and could see that she had created a co-dependent relationship with her partner. She recognized that she had recreated her parents' pattern and began to put in place processes to change this. Her therapy continued for seven months and, in this time, she was able to move to a much more adult relationship in her marriage, had negotiated more flexible working hours, and had begun to make lifestyle changes to take care of herself.

Leila

Leila self-referred for therapy to resolve issues in her current relationship. She described feelings of victimization, loneliness, being taken advantage of, and feeling let down.

Her early childhood history in a traditional Indian family included a happy marriage for her parents. Her aunts were her main carers, and she described a loving relationship with them. She had good memories up to the age of three, when she was admitted to hospital. She was required to stay in hospital for three months following an accident, and during this time had surgery a number of times.

She had a history of family breakdown: she was divorced, and had only limited access to her son and daughter, she had lost a child through cot death when the child was only a few days old. Her husband had been violent towards her, and she identified this as a repeating pattern from her childhood, where her brothers had regularly bullied her, and were violent to her, her mother, and her sister. Her mother was also violent towards her as she got older.

She had experienced periods of depression since her marriage breakdown and had been on antidepressants. She had taken them for only a short period of time, and had stopped them as they appeared to not be working. She described feeling let down regularly in relationships, often over very minor things. For example, a plumber had agreed to call at the weekend, and had not turned up. Her current relationship was experiencing difficulties, and she felt that he was selfish because he would not spend all of his spare time with her.

She was able to contain this feeling to her personal and family relationships, and had been successful in creating a career for herself where she was able to form strong and positive relationships in her business life. She had a good relationship with her sisters, and also had friends that she was close to.

Leila had a history that resonated with some elements of resistant or ambivalent attachment. It was unclear how much of this was present prior to her admission to hospital at the age of three and how much stemmed from this experience. She was a very pleasant client to work with and was also extremely self reliant; I found it took some time to establish a high level of rapport with her, and to open up a dialogue of trust and responsiveness.

Her current relationship was turbulent, with regular break-ups and getting back together. Her relationship history was chequered; her parents had expected her to have an arranged marriage, and she was introduced to suitors from an early age. Her first boyfriend was rejected by her parents, and she married her next boyfriend, who did not meet with her parents' approval. She also lost contact with her aunts at this time, as it was felt that she had disgraced the family. She was married for nine years, and in this time experienced domestic violence and the loss of a child. She had two children, and her husband ensured that she only had limited access to them following their divorce. She still experienced distress over this, and was particularly hurt that her oldest child still blamed her for leaving the marriage. Subsequent to her marriage breakdown, she had been in two relationships, both with very caring men who wanted to have children. She felt that she could not commit to either of these men, both of whom she described as loving, and had entered into her current relationship in the last year.

She had sought therapy after her marriage breakdown and also after the death of her child, and had found this helpful. She was in therapy with me for only a short period of time, and I used only NLPt. She recognized that she had low self-esteem and would seek constant reassurance from her partner that she was all right. She found it difficult to be present in a relationship, and reported her emotions being like a roller coaster of feeling nothing, to then feeling overwhelmed with anxiety, to then feeling head over heels in love.

As we continued in therapy, she spent more time experiencing and making sense of her time in hospital as a young child. She recalled hearing a doctor say to her mother, "You will be lucky if she is still alive tomorrow", and reports being very frightened in case she did die. She reflected on this and connected this to the feeling of being abandoned that was a recurring theme in her subsequent relationships. We spent time on inner child work, reconnecting her to dissociated aspects of her neurology, and she experienced and resolved great feelings of loss for the childhood that she had missed, and also the childhood of the child who had died, as well as her children whom she saw very little of.

My role as a therapist was limited to containing and listening to her story. She had developed strategies for self-healing and was able to take on learnings in therapy without developing an overly strong attachment relationship to me. I ensured that I left responsibility for change with Leila, resourcing her sufficiently so that she could self-soothe. Since leaving therapy, she has continued to read widely on psychological perspectives of her life, and has continued to do inner child work with her abandoned self. From an attachment perspective, this client has a good capacity for self-parenting and is managing extremely well with some very difficult circumstances in her past and current life. She has now reframed her relationships with men and is able to form intimate relationships on an equal power basis.

Emily

Emily self referred to therapy via her friend, who had also attended for therapy with me. She was working as a nurse and was experiencing difficulties with her mother, who had recently become ill and was making massive demands on her time, emotions, and energy. As a single parent of an adolescent teenage son, she was becoming increasingly stressed and was seeking help to enable her to cope. Her mother had become ill two years prior to her seeing me, and she felt that she was in a never ending cycle of looking after her mother, and then going to work to look after other people. She also talked about losing her partner through suicide four years previously, and felt that she had not had time to grieve for him. She could only see her life disappearing and had no hope for a future.

On initial presentation, it appeared that Emily was experiencing reactive depression and was in overwhelm because of life circumstances. There appeared to be nothing that would indicate that she had any attachment problems. She was bright, lively, and very well presented. Even as she described the overwhelm that she was experiencing in her life, she did it while laughing and smiling. I found myself laughing alongside her and, after she left her first session, reflected on it and wondered why I felt so happy about her sad life story. In avoidant attachment patterns, the individual gives an external appearance of all being well, while underneath high levels of anxiety and diminished sense of self occur.

When Emily returned for her next session, I elicited her early history. She was the youngest of three children, her brother had schizophrenia, and her sister was married to an abusive man. Her mother was psychologically unstable and had a history of self harm and physically abusing her husband. By the time Emily was eight, she was also subject to her mother's violent and verbally abusive episodes. She married at eighteen to escape from home and quickly became pregnant. She left the marriage after five years, and straight away entered into another relationship with an abusive man. She tried to end the relationship a number of times, but he kept "wheedling" his way back. After she finally ended the relationship, she met and married someone else. He quickly became violent, and she left that relationship after two years. Her next relationship was with a nurse, who went on to kill himself. After this relationship, she met her next partner, who went on to kill himself after four years of being together. As she relayed this history to me, she continued to laugh and smile and act as if it was completely normal.

Her history and also her telling of the history were indicative of avoidant attachment. She always tried to make me feel good during her sessions in therapy, and would regularly compliment me on various things. I challenged her on this early on in the therapy, and quickly reached a place where she was ready to work on the issues that she presented. She had a high degree of insight, and although she was anxious that she may feel overwhelmed if she were to access her feelings, she was prepared to work on it. She recognized her attachment pattern and asked for references so that she could read further about it. She described feeling always constrained and held back, as if she could not breathe. We used some anchoring processes (Chapter Five) to access more resourceful states, and we went on to discuss how she felt in her childhood. She picked up the blanket that was covering the back of her chair and wrapped it round her, saying that it was like being smothered in a blanket with no room to move. As she pulled the blanket tighter around herself, I used one of Dilt's processes (1987–2005, pp. 6–7) to enable her to access additional resources that would have allowed her to free her neurology from being constrained. She practised the movement a number of times, and, as she did this, her emotions released and she described it as feeling as if she was going to fly. She left that session feeling freer than she had ever felt, and when she returned the following week, she told me that she had signed up for dancing classes and could not stop her body from wanting to move. She ended therapy after another two sessions, and made contact with me after two years. She had got married and was loving every minute of life, able to feel the ups and the downs of life and stay fully associated. She still danced regularly and had finally been able to free herself from the constraints that had kept her tied to her mother.

Sue

I was contacted by Sue as she was beginning to think about returning to work after a long period with ME (myalgic encephalitis). She described feeling trapped and guilty with regard to her mother, and considered that she had let her mother down because she was the one who now needed care because of ME.

Her childhood story consisted of her father leaving the family when she was of pre-school age, and her mother being left with financial problems and little to live for. She described becoming everything to her mother, with this often being coupled with her mother blaming her and saying she was just like her father. She had two older siblings who had left home, so she reports that she always felt the guilt and responsibility for her father leaving and thought that this may have had an impact on her health. Her mother needed to work, and for much of Sue's childhood held down two jobs. Sue was looked after by an aunt and uncle, and describes this as a functional relationship rather than it being caring. Sue had developed asthma and eczema in her early childhood, and regularly required hospitalization. Her mother would accuse her of playing on things and Sue would sometimes become so ill that she had to call on a neighbour and get her to take her to hospital.

Sue made an attempt to leave home when she was eighteen, and soon found that her mother became infirm with a long term disability, which meant that Sue was constantly being called back home and found her guilt getting worse, as she could not enjoy life while her mother needed her so much. She attempted to continue with her travels abroad, but, however, found the guilt too much and returned home to live with her mother.

I asked Sue to describe her history of relationships. She had been in a number of long-term relationships, all of which had a recurring theme or pattern of emotional avoidance.

Her first boyfriend was someone whom she was at school with, which she described as a "typical" early boyfriend relationship. She met her next boyfriend as she was about to go to university; she described him as being very possessive, yet at the same time very uncaring. She told a story of how one of her pets had died, and he thought she was being silly getting upset about it. Her next boyfriend was more of a friend than anything else, and the relationship drifted along for a period of time. Her next partner was twelve years older than Sue. She described him as a father figure, and she quickly married him. Even leading up to the wedding, he would regularly put her down and accuse her of being ugly and overweight, and although she knew it was the wrong thing to do to marry him, she went ahead with the wedding and they separated after only six months. Her next partner was again twelve years older than her. He wanted to marry Sue, but she felt that she could not go through the same thing again and, even if their relationship survived, she rationalized that he would die before her and she would end up with a broken heart. Her next partner was married, and although he said he would leave his wife for Sue, he failed to do this, and Sue eventually ended the relationship. After this relationship, Sue fell in love very quickly with someone that she describes as the nicest person in the world, at which point she decided to commence her travels again, which resulted in the relationship ending. As she reflected on these relationships, she summed up her thoughts with the words, "I can't imagine why a man would love me."

Sue had a very high degree of insight in therapy and worked quickly over the space of five hours to reflect and consider how she might respond differently in relationships. She recognized that she had an avoidant attachment pattern, and we spent some time looking at how she might manage her relationship with her mother more effectively so that she could start to separate and develop a more fulfilling life for herself. Therapy with Sue ended at this point, and I heard no more from her for three years.

When she made contact again, she had managed to move away from home and was working abroad. She still felt guilty about her mother and wanted to do some work on managing her triggered responses to her mother, who was very good at pressing her buttons and causing her to react with rage. We did some work on her inner child, who was experiencing intense anger towards her mother. I then did not see Sue again for another year. I recognized that this was possibly part of Sue's avoidant process, and at the same time respected her clear desire to manage things by herself.

She returned for therapy a year later, and was much more in touch with her feelings. She described herself as being in a "glass box—I can see and interact with my environment, but I cannot feel anything. I feel safe in the glass box, but also isolated, lonely, and depressed. My box is my prison, but also my protector . . . the protector being more important. I am disconnected from my feelings, of both happiness and laughter to sadness. The only time I feel safe to reconnect and feel is with my animals, whom I adore and love totally." She then went on to describe her reflections on her relationships with men. "When I do meet new people (especially men) I generally follow the same pattern as follows:

> Stunned—unable to say anything through fear of saying the wrong thing.
> In a state of paralysis—unable to engage in conversation.
> Stupid—anything about me seems insignificant (in my eyes)— my skills, knowledge, thoughts, ideas, passion, abilities, looks, and knowledge.
> Fearful—"just get me out of here".
> Desire to leave and be on my own, then unhappy I am on my own—I often cry.
> When I hear good things said to me (about me) I feel totally embarrassed, but also doubt the sincerity of the speaker, unless they are a good friend.

Sue had obviously spent a lot of time over the last year reflecting on her own process and becoming more consciously aware of the strategies that she was using to keep herself safe in relationships. We worked very quickly in therapy over a couple of sessions and Sue returned to her job abroad, agreeing to keep in contact with me via email. We did this intermittently, and she was able to continue her therapy through this form of dialogue. Her levels of awareness increased, and she tasked herself to develop more permanent relationships where she was based. As she progressed her own self-reflection, she sent me an email that summarized her early developmental life. "When I was born, my dad was rarely around as he went away to work, leaving mum with myself and my older siblings. I have no recollection of him up to age four. Mum, having to cope with everything, left me for long periods on my own in a pram; I remember the excitement of a neighbour peeping through the window to see if I was OK. Plus, I remember rocking the pram so hard until it tipped up, and I fell asleep upside down in the hood. Oh, and rocking the pram over to the wall and peeling off the wallpaper and throwing books out of the bookshelf. I also remember the frustration and anger at being trapped in that bloody pram, but no matter how hard I tried I could not get free. I still feel like this now. . . . Nothing then until giving the cats and dogs away. I was about four. I remember getting into the van with dad and driving to re-home the animals. I was devastated because I loved them. Then mum and dad arguing (the only time I recall, and actually mum says it was possibly their only argument). Then going to the tip and throwing my plastic car in whilst mum threw in an old mug whilst crying. Then we lived with my aunt and uncle for a while. Dad returned when I was seven and brought me a doll and new coat. He lived for three weeks in the pub across the road and I was not allowed to tell anyone he was my dad. He broke my doll and then he left, and I never saw him again."

As Sue continued her writing she concluded with the comments, "Just writing this is opening up a range of feelings of deep, deep hurt, and it is time I faced it otherwise I shall stay stuck." She returned for further therapy over four hours when she was next on her visits to the UK, and worked very hard with the feelings of hurt that she was experiencing.

I last saw Sue five years after she first consulted me for therapy. She has come a long way in this time and is now able to self-soothe, is in a relationship where she can take things slowly and enjoy feeling affection for and with the other person. She has returned to the UK to live and has established some friendships that are supportive of her and her needs. She has maintained her relationship with her mother, albeit at a healthy distance, and although she sometimes feels guilty about her mother, she no longer allows it to play a major part in her life.

Mary

Mary is an interesting client in that she is probably one of the most long-term clients that I have seen for therapy, although I have never seen her for more than four sequential sessions of therapy, and sometimes it is only one session or email contact. I have supported her for the past nine years, and in this time her therapy has been intermittent and consisted mainly of my containment of her anxious state. She utilizes therapy as a form of soothing when her thoughts begin to run away with her and she becomes highly anxious and self-critical.

Mary self-referred because of increasing levels of self doubt, which was evidenced through a constant internal critic. She was a pleasant lady, very polite, described herself as needing a dominant male around her (her husband), and not able to manage well on her own. She described basing all her decisions according to whether it would please her husband or not, she was unable to say whether she liked herself or not, and was not sure if she knew what love was. She was finding it increasingly difficult to stay quiet in the relationship, and this was leading to alternating internal responses of anger towards her husband and then feeling guilty and self-critical because she should accept all that he did for her.

She was a highly cognitive lady, so I decided to focus on helping her to gain insight and understanding of her values for her relationship. Her values were:

- *respect*—based on not being worthy and needing to respect others as a way of gaining self-worth;
- *trust*—which again was based on a lack of self-worth;
- *friendship*—she was unable to identify what was important to her about this and said that she often felt used by others;
- *similar interests*—based on avoiding tension in the relationship;
- *togetherness*—which enabled her to gain more confidence as she did not feel worthy;
- *complete with each other*—where she was fearful that the relationship might not survive;
- *happiness*—driven by an underlying unhappiness and unrest, which was caused by her failure to make something of herself;
- *everything is right*—which included managing to cope with criticism or "brickbats" which were part of every day life in her relationship
- *oneness*—managing to cope in a crisis and when things aren't going well.

I asked Mary to describe some of her history and she said she viewed her life as if she was looking at it through a camera: "This is how it is supposed to be, but I don't feel anything." She recalled her early childhood: she was the eldest of four children and remembers being there after her two youngest siblings were born, both boys, and thinking to herself how happy her parents were because they now had a son. She was bullied at school and used to wet herself occasionally. She was a late walker and can remember her father smacking her and leaving bruises from a young age. She recalls always seeking praise when she was a child, and would often not go to bed until she had managed to get praised for something, which would resonate with resistant or ambivalent attachment. We worked for a period of six sessions, over which time her values in her relationship had changed to a more balanced motivation and a greater sense of self in the relationship. She now wanted a relationship that was driven by:

- *equal footing;*
- *love;*
- *respect*—which was now more associated towards mutual and equal respect and admiration
- *trust;*
- *I am important.*

Mary then left therapy for a period of six months and made contact again because she was feeling full of hate, which she saw as irrational and based on the fact that she had to keep herself clean and tidy. She had left the previous therapy wanting to be herself and, as she stepped out into this in her relationship, this caused friction, and she was now projecting her anger and hate towards her husband. She begrudged the work that she felt she had to do in keeping the house tidy and wanted to start to do things for herself. We worked on her feelings of inferiority that were driving this emotion, and she was able to reset her goals towards creating more time for herself. She left with some very cognitive actions and I next heard from her later that year. She contacted me by email to share a realization that she had: "Yesterday I was in town and suddenly I was hit by something that resembled a thunderbolt. I had been busy at work and then had to visit a relative and then had a whole load of jobs to do. It dawned on me that I had left something at work. So I had to go back and get it before I could get on with everything else. As I drove back, the thought came to me that I wanted to retire—with effect from today! I wanted to drop every-thing—even all form filling, and any trivia. All I wanted to do was sit and do my sewing and garden, as and when I wanted to! As I began to think all this through, I realized that what I really wanted was some time for ME! And yesterday I didn't get any. Why did this come to me? By bedtime, my head was pounding and I had drunk gallons of water. One of my children rang from university and said could I collect them early from university, I said not, that I had too much work on. A little bit of me felt guilty, because we could have had a good chat, but because the weather is good, I could be in the garden. The garden would be sheer pleasure—time for me to indulge in something that I enjoy and time to think whilst I am working. You have helped me clear so much baggage that I think this thought could come to the surface unbidden."

Two weeks later I received another email from Mary. "This morning another bombshell dropped—this time it was given to me. Up to now, I have been working part time, and in the next few months, I have the opportunity to either go full time or reduce my hours further because of a restructure in our department. The full time has benefits, promotion, more money etc, the part time means less responsibility but also a lesser job. Which one do I want? I have to decide by first thing tomorrow. I'm going home to talk to my husband, though I know he won't give me the answer. He will outline all the pros and cons and leave me to decide. You can't make the final decision for me either." Mary went on to reduce her hours.

I next heard from her later that year. She was starting to address some of the sexual aspects of her relationship, which mirrored the developmental processing that she was doing. She was beginning to assert herself in her relationship and this was inevitably begin-ning to surface some areas of conflict. She worked through these issues over three sessions and she reported, "For years I used to cry and not know how to approach my husband . . . I had an off day and had a good cry and could tell him that I was still frightened of him. I am finding I need to approach him about issues that I used to avoid on occasions—as I said 'trying to find the courage to speak to him'." Mary made contact again nine months later via email and reported a series of family deaths of elderly relatives. She had been starting to feel down again and was considering contacting me, but suddenly experienced a realization. "I realized that life is worth living and that I had got a lot to live for. My husband's problem was not mine and if he could not cope with my grief then he needed to learn how to and, as you have said before, I am the one with the power in the relationship. I realized that if I wanted to get our relationship back on track then I had to do something about it. I have, and it is now better than it has been for the last three weeks, but he is still reluctant to hold me and give me a cuddle." Mary was demonstrating a higher level of coping and also a recognition of her own sense of self separate from the other, something that she had been unable to do early in her therapy.

Since this time, Mary has stayed in occasional contact via email and has seen me twice for short sessions of therapy. Her ambivalence has resolved and she is much more able to state her needs in a relationship without become agitated and actively seeking attention. Although we have maintained a loose therapeutic relationship over nine years in total, she has only seen me for eighteen sessions of therapy. She has needed to know that I am available, and sometimes makes contact just by sending me jokes by email; however, her ability to be self-contained is marked since her first session in therapy, and she now enjoys life and can be on her own for long periods of time.

CHAPTER SEVEN

Conclusions

W ithin this book, I have reviewed each of the brief therapies, that is, existing modalities of therapy that are
usually delivered in twenty sessions or less, and have
included a significant evidence base for the modalities as they relate
to attachment disorder. I have not been exhaustive in my inclusions
and, at the same time, recognize and appreciate that I am not a
natural researcher, therefore any omissions or oversights are not
deliberate. I have concluded this book with a summary review of
existing psychotherapy research into this area, and recommendations for ongoing clinical practice.

Research evidence base

There is a significant evidence base for the role of brief therapies in
working with attachment disorder. Attachment disorder can appear
in a number of guises within therapy and can manifest wherever
individuals consider themselves in relation to the other in a relationship. Shaver, Belsky, and Brennan (2007) have used the Adult
Assessment Interview to study the state of mind with respect to

attachment and have identified a number of domains where attachment related problems may manifest. These include: idealizing of the mother or father figure in light of conflicting evidence; downplaying the importance of attachment relationships; lack of memory for specific examples of attachment experiences; passivity of speech; metacognitive monitoring; irrational discourse; lack of coherence of mind with episodic gaps in semantic memory; defences; unresolved mourning or trauma; fear of loss of one's own child; anger to each parent. Many of these domains also occur in fear and phobia related disorders, relationship difficulties, depression, anxiety, and borderline personality disorder. It would, therefore, be difficult to clearly determine if an individual has attachment disorder; rather, it is the degree that they can successfully relate to others that may be the desired outcome in therapy.

Of the therapies reviewed, several have a strong evidence base for working with attachment-related problems.

A number of studies are currently being conducted assessing the effectiveness of CAT in working with patients with borderline personality disorder. It is interesting to note that individuals such as Kellett are investigating a systemic approach to managing relationships with this particularly difficult group and is beginning to find evidence of an improvement in the relationship where both staff and patients take responsibility for the relationship. One of the principles of CAT is to enable the working through of re-enactments within the therapy.

CBT has demonstrated that it can be effective in clients with attachment avoidance and depressive symptoms compared to interpersonal therapy (McBride, Atkinson, Quilty, & Bagby, 2006), whereas a comparative study with anxious adolescents demonstrated equivalent outcomes when CBT was combined with family therapy.

EMDR is probably one of the most effective evidence-based therapies for working with attachment disorders. Van der Kolk (2005), Shapiro and Brown (2006), Madrid, Skolek, and Shapiro (2006) and Soberman, Greenwald, and Rule, (2002) were all able to demonstrate effective outcomes in working with attachment specific problems across a range of client groups.

NLPt has demonstrated effectiveness in enabling self-care behaviours (Crandell, 1989), and de Miranda and colleagues (1999) were able to demonstrate positive changes in the home environment when NLP was used with mothers in a shanty town area.

Gonzalez and colleagues' (2004) meta-analysis of REBT has demonstrated the effectiveness of the approach in young children with disruptive behaviour patterns, a precursor to attachment related symptoms in later life.

SFBT, through a meta-analysis by Gingerich and Eisengart (2000), has demonstrated support for the modality for a range of conditions, including depression, opposition disorder, parent–child conflict, prison, recidivism, adolescent offending, marital relationships, and addiction problems. There is a significant case study evidence base in Nardone and Portelli's (2005) and Nardone and Watzlawick's (2002) studies over ten years of 3482 cases with a range of attachment indicative pathologies, resulting in an 88% success rate.

Three of the therapies have no empirical evidence base: Ericksonian therapy, self relations therapy, and provocative therapy. Yet, of these three, Ericksonian therapy closely matches the requirements of Schore in his review of the principles of psychotherapeutic treatment for those with affective disorders, and self relations is the closest therapy to both MacLean's theory of the triune brain and emotions, and meets most of Schore's requirements. Evidence base in both of these therapies is required to enable them to take their place in empirically sound therapies.

Merging neuroscience with psychotherapy

Schore (2003a,b), Gerhardt (2004), and Cozolino (2002), have all brought a neuroscience perspective to psychotherapy. Schore has provided a comprehensive review of the role that affect regulation has in supporting or denying a positive sense of self. Gerhardt has provided a focus from the developing brain of the infant and the role that the mother's ability to attune to the infant has in shaping the baby's brain. Cozolino has further developed many neuroscience and psychology studies to provide a perspective on the role of neuroscience in psychotherapy and particularly psychopathology.

Siegel (1999) has identified that individuals who demonstrate secure attachment and autonomous functioning have a high degree of integration between cognitive and emotional neurological networks, whereas individuals who have attachment problems tend to repeat these patterns in adulthood (Brennan & Shaver, 1995; Hazan & Shaver, 1990). Schore (1994) proposes that the structures for attachment-based problems arise in the orbitofrontal cortex, which MacLean (1970) identifies as the area of the brain responsible for object permanence, as well as the centre for mirror neurons. In his later work on affect regulation and repair of the self, Schore (2003a) recommends certain principles within the therapy process to aid affect regulation and repair.

1. *Conceptualization of self psychopathology as deficits of affect regulation—formulation of a treatment model matched to developmental level.*
    CAT, Ericksonian therapy, NLPt, and self relations therapy all work at the developmental level of the client.
    CAT supports the client to recognize and work with patterns of behaviour, including the opportunity to work through re-enactments of early trauma in therapy.
    Ericksonian therapy works with the presenting problem as it is represented by the client and uses unconscious linking to aid accessing of more resourceful states (Rosen, 1992).
    NLPt is based in behavioural modelling and supports the client to model out both useful and unuseful strategies of behaviour. This process enables the client to model to themselves more effective patterns of behaviour.
    Self relations therapy views psychological disturbance as a shift in identity that can be used for growth in the individual. It supports and validates the person to acknowledge and work with somatized and cognitive elements of processing.
2. *Model of right brain interactive affect regulation as fundamental process of psychobiological development and psychotherapeutic treatment.*
    CAT, EMDR, Ericksonian therapy, NLPt, and provocative therapy all provide models of right brain interactive and empowering processes to aid psychobiological development.
    CAT works co-operatively with the client, enabling re-enactments to occur and be managed within therapy.
    EMDR directs its attention to the neurological, somatic, and cognitive elements of disturbance, using a combination of

visualization, eye movement, mindfulness and dual attention to assist neurological change.

Ericksonian therapy utilizes indirect and permissive communication to the right brain to assist accessing of inner resources to effect change.

NLPt works with a combination of neurological and linguistic reframes to enable accessing of more effective resources, often held within the unconscious.

Provocative therapy focuses on generalized and conditioned responses and uses a variety of means of unconscious and conscious communication to facilitate change in the individual.

3. *Focus on identification and integration of non-conscious biological states of mind/body.*

CAT, EMDR, NLPt, REBT, SFBT, self relations therapy all use a variety of means to enable both identification and integration of non-conscious biological states of mind/body. Some of the therapies, such as CAT, NLPt, REBT, and SFBT have more emphasis on the cognitive elements, whereas self relations therapy and EMDR have a much greater reliance on non-conscious biological states.

4. *Understanding of therapeutic empathy, right brain non-verbal psychobiological attunement.*

Use of affect synchronizing transactions that forges the patient's attachment to the therapist.

Although therapeutic empathy is probably common across most therapies, it is a particular component of CAT, Ericksonian therapy, REBT, and self relations therapy. CAT works positively with transference and countertransference, and REBT assumes a level of healthy functioning that means that the client can work in a time limited way and manage the attachment relationship with the therapist.

Ericksonian therapy and self relations therapy, which emerged from Gilligan's modelling of Erickson, both require psychobiological attunement on behalf of the therapist. Erickson would use unconscious attunement throughout all of his work with his clients, and Gilligan works with attunement by reflecting back to clients their somatically held experiences.

5. *Operational definition of therapeutic alliance in terms of non-conscious yet mutually reciprocal influences. The patient's capacity*

for attachment combines with the therapist's contingently responsive facilitating behaviours.
Each of the therapies of CAT, Ericksonian therapy, REBT, self relations therapy and SFBT recognize the need for reciprocal non-conscious attunement. SFBT and Ericksonian therapy would both work only with positive and empowering processes with the client.

6. *Therapist is experienced as being in a state of vitalizing attunement to the patient, resonating with the patient's right brain.*
CAT works with the positive aspects of transference and countertransference, and avoids recognition of the more psychoanalytic perspective of resistance.
Ericksonian and self relations therapy both consider attunement to the client as core to the therapy, with much of the work being done through non-verbal processes (Gilligan, 1997, 2004; Rosen, 1992).

7. *Stress on dysregulated right brain "primitive affects" and identification of unconscious dissociated affects that were never developmentally interactively regulated, rather than analysis of unconscious resistance and disavowal of repressed affect.*
Permission, acknowledgement, and validation of affective states are key elements of CAT, EMDR, Ericksonian therapy, NLPt, provocative therapy, REBT, and self relations therapy. None of the these models of therapy recognizes resistance as a negative process and all have created ways to recognize the positive intention or aspect of what others might refer to as resistance in therapy.

8. *Awareness of clinician's right hemispheric countertransferential visceral–somatic responses to the patient's transferential affects. Attention to the intensity, duration, frequency, and lability of the patient's internal state.*
Only CAT and self relations therapy recognize the role of the clinician's visceral–somatic responses to the patient's transferential affects. CAT does this to a degree by enabling the re-enactment of affective states within the therapy, and self relations therapy works closely with the somatic, relational, and generative minds, with the therapist often mirroring aspects of the negated or fragmented self.

9. *Moment-to-moment tracking of content-associated subtle and dramatic shifts in arousal and state in patient narratives. Identification of non-conscious "hot" cognitions that dysregulate self function.*

   All of the brief therapies except for EMDR utilize processes that track the content-associated changes in arousal and state. EMDR focuses more on the non-content neurobiological changes that occur; however, clients may report free association images and thoughts if they wish. "Hot" cognitions are also considered by all of the therapies except for EMDR, with some therapies such as REBT, CBT, and NLPt working with the semantic meaning of words to a lesser or greater degree.

10. *Awareness of dyadically triggered, non-verbal shame dynamics, and co-creation of interpersonal context within the therapeutic alliance that allows for deeper self revelation.*

   Many of the brief therapies remain outside of the processes that uncover dyadically triggered shame dynamics. The co-created interpersonal context is utilized to a high degree in CAT, with Kellett identifying the effect that staff involvement can have on effecting therapeutic outcome. Ericksonian therapy and self relations therapy both view the co-created context as fundamental to the therapy process. NLPt, through the model of Gawler-Wright (2004, 2007), who is also an Ericksonian therapist, holds true to the notion of a co-created reality.

11. *Conception of defence mechanisms as non-conscious strategies of emotional regulation for avoiding, minimizing, or converting affects that are intolerable. Emphasis on dissociation and projective identification as ways of defending against intense affects that can disorganize the self system.*

   Only Ericksonian therapy and self relations therapy utilize unconscious strategies of avoidance as a way of managing affects. Erickson was excellent at employing this process in his therapy and regularly tasked clients to manage their affects through more tolerable and acceptable ways (Haley, 1973).

12. *Uncovering of insecure attachment histories imprinted and stored as right hemispheric working models.*

   Very few of the models of therapy include the uncovering of attachment histories. CAT, which emerged from the analytic tradition, places emphasis on understanding early patterns of behaviour, as does REBT. Self relations therapy approaches it differently, in that imprinting models are accessed through the relational mind and then worked with in the generative mind. These are often non-cognitive in design, whereas CAT and REBT place greater cognitive emphasis on the imprinting of models.

One of the weaknesses of the other approaches is the lack of exploration or recognition of early attachment relationships.

13. *Identification of early-forming, rapid-acting, and non-conscious right brain perceptual biases for detecting threatening social stimuli. Enactments occur as stress coping strategies.*

All of the brief therapy approaches pay attention to behaviours that are a response to threatening social stimuli. Some therapies, such as CBT, see these as cognitively driven strategies, whereas most of the other therapies make links to the non-conscious and emotional factors that are at play. SFBT is an exception, in that it tends to look for exceptions to these responses and accesses neurological and cognitive pathways when the problem pattern is not running, leading to a preferred future.

14. *Appreciation of the centrality of interactive repair as a therapeutic mechanism—facilitates mutual regulation of affective homeostasis.*

Much of Erickson's work involved the return to homeostasis, and this is reflected in Gilligan's developmental work from Erickson. CAT also recognizes the role of interactive repair as a mechanism of therapeutic change and again, Kellett's (2009) study is beginning to demonstrate this.

15. *Understanding that the therapist's affect tolerance is a critical factor determining the range, types, and intensities of emotions that are explored or disavowed in the therapy.*

None of the therapies appears to place the therapist's affect tolerance at the centre of the therapeutic process, with some therapies negating any influence that the role of the therapist has on effecting change. It is an interesting point that some of the more analytic approaches to therapy are beginning to harness and utilize approaches such as EMDR in their work (Mollon, 2004).

16. *Emphasis on the process rather than genetic interpretations. Attention to right hemisphere emotion communicating as well as linguistic content of interpretations.*
All of the therapies except for CAT and CBT place a high degree of emphasis on the process rather than interpretation. Therapies such as NLPt and REBT also consider the linguistic content equivalent to the emotional component. For some of the therapies, there is greater emphasis on emotional content, such as EMDR; however, most of the brief therapies are effective at linking emotion to cognition, potentially creating possibility for neuropsychological repair.

17. *Directing of therapeutic technique towards the elevation of emotions from a primitive form to a mature symbolic representation level. Creation of self reflective position that can appraise significance and meaning of affects.*
All of the therapies except for EMDR facilitate the transition from primitive emotional response to a mature, symbolic representation level. As each of the therapies are mostly outcome focused, clients are able to reflect on and make meaning of their change as they progress through therapy. It is unclear how this process occurs in EMDR.

18. *Growth facilitating therapeutic environment that enables a modulated self system that can integrate a broad range of affects.*
Each of the therapies of CAT, Ericksonian therapy, NLPt, REBT, self relations therapy, and SFBT have at their core a positive and resourcing attitude to therapy with clients. Behaviours are viewed in context, and for some therapies, such as NLPt, self relations therapy, and SFBT, the person is always viewed as more than their behaviour. The aim of each of these therapies is to assist the client to access more choice and a corresponding ability to manage affects with a greater degree of resilience.

19. *Restoration and expansion of patient's capacity for self-regulation. Flexibly regulate emotional states in interactions with others. Autonomous autoregulation and resilience to shift between these two modes.*
The underlying principles of CAT, Ericksonian therapy, NLPt, provocative therapy, REBT, and SFBT are that the client is supported towards a greater capacity for self regulation. Each of these therapies also considers the subjective nature of the client and the place that the other has in the client's overall

view. By reframing and gaining an increased ability to self regulate, the client re-enters the world with a greater capacity for managing themselves in relation to others and with a higher degree of personal autonomy.

20. *Long term goal of reorganizing insecure internal working models into earned secure models. Development of the ability to maintain a coherent, continuous and unified sense of self.*
The therapies of CAT, Ericksonian therapy, NLPt, provocative therapy, REBT, self relations therapy, and SFBT all have a model of the internal structure of a client's world. Within this, there is also the recognition and assumption that the client can develop a more coherent, continuous, and unified sense of self.

Summary

All of the brief therapies offer the potential for psychological growth and repair in attachment disorder. Each of them, to a greater or lesser extent, are using theories within neuroscience to assist change. For some therapies, such as EMDR and NLPt, this is a deliberate and planned approach to therapy; for others, it is clearly occurring, although the therapies do not claim to be using neuroscience to affect repair.

There is a need for extensive research into this area. This would ideally include and not be limited to:

- effectiveness of comparative therapies in treating attachment disorders;
- longitudinal studies of the effects of brief therapies in specific client groups;
- the role of the therapist in creating the potential for positive affect;
- self-regulating systems of the therapist in repair of attachment disorders with clients.

Into each life some confusion should come . . . and also some enlightenment.

And my voice goes everywhere with you, and changes into the voice of your parents, your teachers, your playmates and the voices of the wind and of the rain . . . [Milton H. Erickson (Zeig, 1980)]

REFERENCES

Abbass, A. A., Hancock, J. T., Henderson, J., & Kisely, S. (2006). Short-term psychodynamic psychotherapies for common mental disorders. *Cochrane Database of Systematic Reviews, 3*, 2008.

Adler, A. (1992) [1927]. *Understanding Human Nature*, C. Brett (Trans.). Oxford: Oneword Publications.

Allen, K. L. (1982). An investigation of the effectiveness of Neuro-linguistic Programming procedures in treating snake phobics. *Dissertation Abstracts International, 43*(3): 861-B.

American Psychiatric Association (2000). *Diagnostic and Statistical Manual of Mental Disorders (DSM-IV)* (2000). 4th edn. Washington, DC: American Psychiatric Association.

Anderson, L., Lewis, G., Araya, R., Elgie, R., Harrison, G., & Proudfoot, J. (2005). Self-help books for depression: how can practitioners and patients make the right choice? *British Journal of General Practice, 55*: 387–392.

Andersson, G., Bergstrom, J., Hollandare, F., Carlbring, P., Kaldo, V., & Ekselius, L. (2005). Internet-based self-help for depression: random-ised controlled trial. *British Journal of Psychiatry, 187*: 456–461.

Andreas, C., & Andreas, S. (1987). *Change Your Mind—And Keep The Change*. Moab, UT: Real People Press.

Antrobus, J. S., Antrobus, J. S., & Singer, J. L. (1964). Eye movements accompanying daydreaming, visual imagery, and thought suppression. *Journal of Abnormal and Social Psychology, 69*: 244–252.

Bandura, A. (1977). *Social Learning Theory.* Englewood Cliffs, NJ: Prentice-Hall.

Beck, A. T. (1963). Thinking and depression: 1. Idiosyncratic content and cognitive distortions. *Archives of General Psychiatry, 9*: 324–333.

Beck, A. T. (1976). *Cognitive Therapy and the Emotional Disorders.* New York: International Universities Press.

Beck, A. T., Rush, A. J., Shaw, B. E., & Emery, G. (1979). *The Cognitive Therapy of Depression.* New York: Guildford Press.

Bennett, D., Parry, G., & Ryle, A. (2006). Resolving threats to the therapeutic alliance in cognitive analytic therapy. *Psychology and Psychotherapy, 79*: 395–418.

Berg, I. K., & Dolan, Y. (2001). *Tales of Solutions: A Collection of Hope Inspiring Stories.* New York: W. W. Norton.

Berg, I. K., & Kelly, S. (2000). *Building Solutions in Child Protection Services.* New York: W. W. Norton.

Berg, I. K., & Reuss, N. (1997). *Solutions Step-by-Step: Substance Abuse Treatment Manual.* New York: W. W. Norton.

Bisson, J., & Andrew, M. (2007). Psychological treatment of post-traumatic stress disorder (PTSD). *Cochrane Database of Systematic Reviews, 3.*

Blatt, S. J., Levy, K. N., & Shaver, P. R. (1988). Attachment styles and parental representations. *Journal of Personality and Social Psychology, 74*: 407–419.

Bond, J. A., Hansell, J., & Shevrin, H. (1987). Locating transference paradigms in psychotherapy transcripts: reliability of relationship episode location in the Core Conflictual Relationship Theme (CCRT) method. *Psychotherapy Research, Practice and Training, American Psychological Association, 24*(4): 736–749.

Bowlby, J. (1951). *Maternal Care and Mental Health.* Geneva: World Health Organisation.

Bowlby, J. (1969). *Attachment and Loss: Vol. 1, Attachment.* London: Hogarth Press.

Bowlby, J. (1973). *Attachment and Loss: Vol. 2, Separation: Anxiety and Anger.* New York: Basic Books.

Bowlby, J. (1980). *Attachment and Loss: Vol. 3, Sadness and Depression.* New York: Basic Books.

Brennan, K. A., & Shaver, P. R. (1995). Dimensions of adult attachment, affect regulation, and romantic relationship functioning. *Personality and Social Psychology Bulletin*, 21(3): 267–283.

Bretherton, I. (1987). New perspectives on attachment relations: security, communication, and internal working models. In: J. Osofsky (Ed.), *Handbook of Infant Development* (pp. 1061–1100). New York: Wiley.

Brief Therapy Practice (accessed 16 February 2008) http://www.brieftherapy.org.uk/whathappens.php.

Carlbring, P., Westling, B. E., Ljungstrand, P., Ekselius, L., & Andersson, G. (2001). Treatment of panic disorder via the internet: a randomized trial of a self-help program. *Behavior Therapy*, 32: 751–764.

Cavanagh, K., & Shapiro, D. A. (2004). Computer treatment for common mental health problems. *Journal of Clinical Psychology*, 60: 239–251.

Chopra, D. (1989). *Quantum Healing: Exploring the Frontiers of Mind/Body Medicine*. New York: Bantam Books.

Christensen, H., Griffiths, K. M., & Jorm, A. F. (2004). Delivering interventions for depression by using the internet: randomised controlled trial. *British Medical Journal*, 328(7434): 1200–1201.

Chugani, H. (1996). Neuroimaging of development nonlinearity and developmental pathologies. In: R. Thatcher, G. Lyon, J. Rumsey, & N. Krasnegor (Eds.), *Developmental Neuroimaging. Mapping the Development of the Brain and Behaviour* (pp. 187–195). San Diego, CA: Academic Press.

Churchill, R., Hunot, V., Corney, R., Knapp, M., McGuire, H., & Tylee, A. (2001). A systematic review of controlled trials of the effectiveness of brief psychological treatments for depression. *Health Technology Assessment*, 5: 1–173.

Clark, D. M., Ehlers, A., Hackmann, A., McManus, F., Fennell, M. J. V., & Waddington, L. (2006). Cognitive therapy versus exposure plus applied relaxation in social phobia: a randomised controlled trial. *Journal of Consulting and Clinical Psychology*, 71: 1058–1067.

Clark, D. M., Ehlers, A., McManus, F., Hackmann, A., Fennell, M., & Campbell, H. (2003). Cognitive therapy versus fluoxetine in generalized social phobia: a randomized placebo-controlled trial. *Journal of Consulting and Clinical Psychology*, 71(6): 1058–1067.

Clark, D. M., Salkovskis, P. M., Hackmann, A., Middleton, H., Anastasiades, P., & Gelder, M. G. (1994). A comparison of cognitive therapy, applied relaxation and imipramine in the treatment of panic disorder. *British Journal of Psychiatry*, 164: 759–769.

Clark, D. M., Salkovskis, P. M., Hackmann, A., Wells, A., Fennell, M., & Ludgate, J. (1998). Two psychological treatments for hypochondriasis: a randomised controlled trial. *British Journal of Psychiatry*, 173: 218–225.

Clark, D. M., Salkovskis, P. M., Hackmann, A., Wells, A., Ludgate, J., & Gelder, M. (1999). Brief cognitive therapy for panic disorder: a randomized controlled trial. *Journal of Consulting and Clinical Psychology*, 67: 583–589.

Cole-Dekte, H., & Kobak, R. (1994). *Attentional Processes in Eating Disorders and Depression: An Attachment Perspective*. Newark: University of Delaware.

Cozolino, L. J. (2002). *The Neuroscience of Psychotherapy. Building and Rebuilding the Human Brain*. New York: W. W. Norton.

Crandell, J. S. (1989). Brief treatment for adult children of alcoholics: accessing resources for self-care. *Psychotherapy: Theory, Research, Practice, Training*, 26(4): 510–513.

Critical Appraisal Skills Programme (1999/2006). Public Health Resource Unit.

Damasio, A. (1994). *Descartes Error. Emotion, Reason and the Human Brain*. New York: Penguin.

David, D., & Avellino, M. (2003). *A Synopsis of Rational–Emotive Behaviour Therapy (REBT): Basic/Fundamental and Applied Research*. Cluj, Romania: Babes-Bolyai University.

Davidson, J. R., Foa, E. B., Huppert, J. D., Keefe, F. J., Franklin, M. E., & Compton, J. S. (2004). Fluoxetine, comprehensive cognitive behavioral therapy, and placebo in generalized social phobia. *Archives of General Psychiatry*, 61(10): 1005–1013.

Davidson, R., & Fox, N. (1982). Asymmetrical brain activity discriminates between positive v. negative affective stimuli in human infants. *Science*, 218: 1235–1237.

DeJong, P., & Berg, I. K. (2001). *Interviewing for Solutions*. Pacific Grove, CA: Brooks/Cole.

de Miranda, C. T., de Paula, C. S., Palma, D., da Silva, E. M. K., Martin, D., & de Nóbrega, F. J. (1999). Impact of the application of neurolinguistic programming to mothers of children enrolled in a day care centre of a shantytown. *Sao Paolo Medical Journal*, 117(2): 63–71.

de Shazer, S. (1991). *Putting Difference to Work*. New York: W. W. Norton.

de Shazer, S. (1994). *Words Were Originally Magic*. New York: W. W. Norton.

de Zulueta, F. (2002). Post-traumatic stress disorder and dissociation. The traumatic stress service in the Maudsley Hospital. In: V. Sinason (Ed.), *Attachment, Trauma and Multiplicity. Working with Dissociative Identity Disorder* (pp. 60–61). Hove: Brunner-Routledge.

Dilts, R. (1987–2005). *The Hero's Journey Handouts*, 25–27 January 2007. Instituut voor Eclectische Psychologie, Nijmegen.

Dilts, R. (1990). *Changing Belief Systems with NLP.* Capitola, CA: Meta Publications.

Dilts, R., & Epstein, T. (1991). *Tools for Dreamers.* Capitola, CA: Meta Publications.

Dilts, R. B., & DeLozier, J. (2000). *Encyclopedia of Systemic Neurolinguistic Programming and NLP New Coding.* Scotts Valley, CA: NLP University Press.

Dobson, K. (1989). A meta-analysis of the efficacy of cognitive therapy for depression. *Journal of Consulting and Clinical Psychology, 57:* 414–420.

Dryden, W. (1996). *Handbook of Individual Therapy.* London: Sage.

Dugas, M. J., Ladouceur, R., Leger, E., Freeston, M. H., Langlois, F., & Provencher, M. D. (2003). Group cognitive–behavioral therapy for generalized anxiety disorder: treatment outcome and long-term follow-up. *Journal of Consulting and Clinical Psychology, 71*(4): 821–825.

Dujovne, B. (1990). Paradoxical sadness or painful love. *American Psychological Association, 27*(3): 475–478.

EANLPt (2008). http://www.eanlpt.org/theoretical.html (accessed 19 January 2008).

Ehlers, A., Clark, D. M., Hackmann, A., McManus, F., & Fennell, M. (2005). Cognitive therapy for post-traumatic stress disorder: Development and evaluation. *Behaviour Research and Therapy, 43:* 413–431.

Ehlers, A., Clark, D. M., Hackmann, A., McManus, F., Fennell, M., & Herbert, C. (2003). A randomized controlled trial of cognitive therapy, a self-help booklet, and repeated assessments as early interventions for posttraumatic stress disorder. *Archives of General Psychiatry, 60*(10): 1024–1032.

Einspruch, E. L., & Forman, B. D. (1985). Observations concerning research literature on neuro-linguistic programming. *Journal of Counselling Psychology, 32*(4): 589–596.

Einspruch, E. L., & Forman, B. D. (1988). Neurolinguistic programming in the treatment of phobias. *Psychotherapy in Private Practice, 6*(1): 91–100.

Ellis, A. (1962). *Reason and Emotion in Psychotherapy*. Seacaucus, NJ: Lyle Stuart.

Erickson, B. A., & Keeney, B. (Eds.) (2006). *Milton H. Erickson, M.D. An American Healer*. Sedona, AZ: Ringing Rocks Press.

Erickson, M. H. (1985). *The Lectures, Seminars and Workshops of Milton H. Erickson. Vol II. Life Reframing in Hypnosis*, E. L. Rossi & M. Ryan (Eds.). New York: Irvington.

Erickson, M. H., & Rossi, E. L. (1979). *Hypnotherapy: An Exploratory Casebook*. New York: Irvington.

Erickson, M. H., & Rossi, E. L. (1989). *The February Man. Evolving Consciousness and Identity in Hypnotherapy*. New York: Brunner Mazel.

Fairbairn, R. (1943). The repression and return of the bad objects (with special reference to the "war neuroses"). In: *Psycho-Analytic Studies of the Personality* (pp. 59–81). London: Routledge and Kegan Paul.

Fairbairn, R. (1946). Object relations and dynamic structure. In: *Psycho-Analytic Studies of the Personality*. London: Routledge and Kegan Paul.

Fairbairn, R. (1952). *Psychoanalytic Studies of the Personality*. London: Routledge and Kegan Paul.

Fals-Stewart, W., Marks, A. P., & Schafer, J. (1993). A comparison of behavioral group therapy and individual behavior therapy in treating obsessive-compulsive disorder. *Journal of Nervous and Mental Disease, 181*(3): 189–193.

Farrelly, F., & Brandsma, J. (1974). *Provocative Therapy*. Cupertino, CA: Meta.

Ferguson, D. M. (1987). The effect of two audiotaped Neurolinguistic Programming (NLP) phobia treatments on public speaking anxiety. *Dissertation Abstracts International.*

Fonagy, P., Leigh, T., Kennedy, R., Mattoon, G., Steele, H., Target, M., Steele, M., & Higgit, A. (1995). The relation of attachment status, psychiatric classsification and response of psychotherapy. *Journal of Consulting and Clinical Psychology, 64*: 22–31.

Forrester, D., Copello, A., Waissbein, C., & Pokhrel, S. (2008). Evaluation of an intensive family preservation service for families affected by parental substance misuse. *Child Abuse Review, 17*(6): 410–426.

Fraley, R. C., Davis, K. E., & Shaver, P. R. (1998). Dismissing avoidance and the defensive organization of emotion, cognition, and behavior. In: J. A. Simpson & W. S. Rholes (Eds.), *Attachment Theory and Close Relationships* (pp. 249–279). New York: Guilford Press.

Froggatt, W. (1997). *The Life That Can Be Yours*. Auckland, NZ: Harper Collins.

Fuchs, C., & Rehm, L. (1977). A self-control behavior therapy program for depression. *Journal of Consulting and Clinical Psychology, 45*: 206–215.

Gallese, V. (2001). The "shared manifold" hypothesis. From mirror neurons to empathy. *Journal of Consciousness Studies, 85*(5–7): 33–50.

Gallese, V., & Goldman, A. (1998). Mirror neurons and the simulation theory of mind reading. *Trends in Cognitive Sciences, 2*: 493–501.

Gallese, V., Fadiga, L., Fogassi, L., & Rizzolatti, G. (1996). Action recognition in the pre-motor cortex. *Brain, 119*: 593–609.

Gawler-Wright, P. (1999). *The Skills of Love*. London: BeeLeaf.

Gawler-Wright, P. (2004). *Intermediate Contemporary Psychotherapy Volume 1*. London: BeeLeaf.

Gawler-Wright, P. (2005). A time machine between your ears. Presentation to the Independent NLP Conference, London.

Gawler-Wright, P. (2006). *Wider Mind; Ericksonian Psychotherapy in Practice*. London: BeeLeaf.

Gawler-Wright, P. (2007). *Intermediate Contemporary Psychotherapy Volume 2, 2007 Edition*. London: BeeLeaf.

Genser-Medlitsch, M., & Schütz, P. (1997). *Does Neuro-Linguistic Psychotherapy Have Effect? New Results Shown in the Extramural Section*. Austria: EANLPt.

Gerhardt, S. (2004). *Why Love Matters. How Affection Shapes a Baby's Brain*. London: Routledge.

Gill, M. M., & Hoffman, I. Z. (1982). A method for studying the analysis of aspects of the patient's experience of the relationship in psychoanalysis and psychotherapy. *Journal of the American Psychoanalytic Association, 30*: 137–167.

Gilligan, S. (1997). *The Courage to Love: Principles & Practices of Self-Relations Psychotherapy*. New York: W. W. Norton.

Gilligan, S. (2004). *Walking in Two Worlds: The Relational Self in Theory, Practice, and Community*. Phoenix: Zeig Tucker.

Gingerich, W. J., & Eisengart, S. (2000). Solution-focused brief therapy: a review of the outcome research. *Family Process, 39*(4): 477–498.

Glaser, B., & Strauss, A. (1967). *The Discovery of Grounded Theory: Strategies for Qualitative Research*. Chicago, IL: Aldine.

Glaser, D. E., Grezes, J. S., Calvo, B., Passingham, R. E., & Haggard, P. (2004). *Functional Imaging of Motor Experience and Expertise During Action Observation*. London: University College Press.

Goldberg, E. (2001). *The Executive Brain. Frontal Lobes and the Civilised Mind*. Oxford: Oxford University Press.

Goleman, D. (2003). *Destructive Emotions: How Can We Overcome Them? A Scientific Dialogue with the Dalai Lama*. New York: Bantam Bell.

Gomez, L. (1997). *An Introduction to Object Relations*. London: Free Association Books.

Gonzalez, J. E., Nelson, J. R., Gutkin, T. B., Saunders, A., Galloway, A., & Shwery, C. S. (2004). Rational emotive therapy with children and adolescents: a meta-analysis. *Journal of Emotional and Behavioral Disorders*, 12(4): 222–235.

Grazebrook, K., Garland, A., & the Board of BABCP (2005). What are cognitive and/or behavioural psychotherapies? Paper prepared for a UKCP/BACP mapping psychotherapy exercise (document available online: http://www.babcp.com/silo/files/what-is-cbt.pdf).

Greenough, W. T., & Black, T. E. (1992). Introduction of brain structure by experience: substrates for cognitive development. In: M. R. Gunnar & C. A. Nelson (Eds.), *Minnesota Symposium on Child Psychology. Volume 24: Developmental Behavioural Neuroscience* (pp. 155–200). Hillsdale, NJ: Lawrence Erlbaum.

Greenough, W. T., Black, T. E., & Wallace, C. S. (1987). Experience and brain development. *Child Development*, 58(3): 539–559.

Hale, R. L. (1986). The effects of Neurolinguistic Programming (NLP) on public speaking anxiety and incompetence. *Dissertation Abstracts International*, 47(5).

Haley, J. (1973). *Uncommon Therapy. The Psychiatric Techniques of Milton H. Erickson. M.D.* New York: W. W. Norton.

Hamer. S., & Collinson, G. (Eds.) (1999). *Achieving Evidence-Based Practice: A Handbook for Practitioners*. London: Bailliere Tindall.

Hart, S. (2008). *Brain, Attachment, Personality. An Introduction to Neuroaffective Development*. London: Karnac.

Hazan, C., & Shaver, P. R. (1990). Love and work: an attachment-theoretical perspective. *Journal of Personality and Social Psychology*, 59(2): 270–280.

Heimberg, R. G., Dodge, C. S., Hope, D. A., Kennedy, C. R., & Zollo, L. J. (1990). Cognitive behavioural group treatment for social phobia: comparison with a credible placebo control. *Cognitive Therapy and Research*, 14: 1–23.

Heimberg, R. G., Liebowitz, M. R., Hope, D. A., Schneier, F. R., Holt, C. S., & Welkowitz, L. A. (1998). Cognitive behavioral group therapy vs phenelzine therapy for social phobia—12-week outcome. *Archives of General Psychiatry*, 55(12): 1133–1141.

Hilsenroth, M., Stein, M., & Pinsker, J. (2007). Social cognition and object relations scale: global rating method (SCORS-G) (3rd edn). Unpublished manuscript. Derner Institute of Advanced Psychological Studies, Adelphi University, Garden City, NY.

Hirai, M., & Clum, G. A. (2006). A meta-analytic study of self-help interventions for anxiety problems. *Behavior Therapy, 37*(2): 99.

Hollander, J., Dawes, G., & Duba, R. (1990–2000). *The Farrelly Factors* www.provocativetherapytraining.com/factors.php (accessed December 2008).

Hollon, S. D., & Beck, A. T. (2004). Cognitive and cognitive behavioural therapies. In: M. J. Lambert (Ed.), *Bergin and Garfield's Handbook of Psychotherapy and Behaviour Change* (5th edn) (pp. 447–492). New York: Wiley.

Hollon, S. D., Thase, M. E., & Markowitz, J. C. (2002). Treatment and prevention of depression. *Psychological Science, 3*(2): 39–77.

House, R., & Loewenthal, D. (Eds.) (2008). *Against and for CBT: Towards a Constructive Dialogue?* Ross-on-Wye: PCCS Books.

James, T. (2003). *Time Line Therapy(r) Practitioner Training.* Series Notes, Vers. 6.26...08/2003.

Kaltenthaler, E., Brazier, J., De Nigris, E., Tumur, I., Ferriter, M., & Beverley, C. (2006). Computerised cognitive behaviour therapy for depression and anxiety update: a systematic review and economic evaluation. *Health Technology Assessment, 10*(33): 1–70.

Kammer, D., Lanver, C., & Schwochow, M. (1997). Controlled treatment of simple phobias with NLP: evaluation of a pilot project. University of Bielefeld, Department of Psychology (unpublished paper).

Kellet, S., Bennett, D., & Ryle, A. (2009). The effectiveness of CAT for borderline personality disorder: the shape of change in routine practice. Unpublished paper. stephen.kellett@barnsleypct.nhs.uk.

Kernberg, O. (1975). *Borderline Conditions and Pathological Narcissism.* New York: Jason Aronson.

Kim, J. S. (2008). Examining the effectiveness of solution-focused brief therapy: a meta-analysis. *Research on Social Work Practice, 18*: 107–116.

Klein, M. (1928). Early stages of the Oedipus complex. In: *Love, Guilt and Reparation.* London: Hogarth (1975).

Klein, M. (1946). Notes on some schizoid mechanisms. *International Journal of Psycho-Analysis, 27*: 99–110.

Klein, M. (1952). Notes on some schizoid mechanisms. In: J. Riviere (Ed.), *Developments in Psychoanalysis.* London: Hogarth.

Klein, M. (1960). *Our Adult World and Its Roots in Infancy*. London: Tavistock.

Knekt, P., & Lindfors, O. (Eds.) (2004). A randomized trial of the effect of four forms of psychotherapy on depressive and anxiety disorders. Design, methods and results on the effectiveness of short-term psychodynamic psychotherapy and solution-focused therapy during a one-year follow-up. *Studies in Social Security and Health, 77*. The Social Incurance Institution, Helsinki.

Knekt, P., Lindfors, O., Härkänen, T., Välikoski, M., Virtala, E., Laaksonen, M. A., Marttunen, M., Kaipainen, M., Renlund, C., and the Helsinki Psychotherapy Study Group (2008). Randomized trial on the effectiveness of long-and short-term psychodynamic psychotherapy and solution-focused therapy on psychiatric symptoms during a 3-year follow-up. *Psychological Medicine, 38*: 689–703.

Kohut, H., & Wolf, E. (1978). The disorders of the self and their treatment: an outline. *International Journal of Psychoanalysis, 59*: 413–424.

Koziey, P. W., & McLeod, G. (1987). Visual-kinesthetic dissociation in treatment of victims of rape (research and practice). *Professional Psychology: Research and Practice, 18*(3): 276–282.

Krugman, M., Kirsch, I., Wickless, C., Milling, L., Golicz, H., & Toth, A. (1985). Neuro-linguistic programming treatment for anxiety: magic or myth? *Journal of Consulting & Clinical Psychology, 53*(4): 526–530.

Ladouceur, R., Dugas, M. J., Freeston, M. H., Leger, E., Gagnon, F., & Thibodeau, N. (2000). Efficacy of a cognitive-behavioural treatment for generalized anxiety disorder: evaluation in a controlled clinical trial. *Journal of Consulting and Clinical Psychology, 68*(6): 957–964.

Lange, A., Rietdijk, D., Hudcovicova, M., van de Ven, J.-P., Schrieken, B., & Emmelkamp, P. M. G. (2003). Interapy: A controlled randomized trial of the standardized treatment of posttraumatic stress through the internet. *Journal of Consulting and Clinical Psychology, 71*(5): 901–909.

Lawley, J., & Tomkins, P. (2005). *Metaphors in Mind. Transformation Through Symbolic Modelling*. Developing Company Press.

Layard, R., Bell, S., Clark, D. M., Knapp, M., Meacher, B., Priebe, S., Thornicroft, G., Turnberg, L., & Wright, B. (2006). *The Depression Report: A New Deal for Depression and Anxiety Disorders*. London: The Centre for Economic Performance's Mental Health Policy Group, London School of Economics.

LeDoux, J. (1998). *The Emotional Brain. The Mysterious Underpinnings of Emotional Life*. London: Weidenfeld & Nicholson.

LeDoux, J. (2001). *Synaptic Self: How Our Brains Become Who We Are*. New York: Viking.

LeDoux, J. (2002). *The Emotional Brain*. London: Weidenfield and Nicholson.

Liberman, M. B. (1984). The treatment of simple phobias with Neurolinguistic Programming techniques. *Dissertation Abstracts International*, *45*(6).

Llewelyn, S. (2009). *A Process Study Evaluating Rupture Repair in CAT, Using an Adolescent Sample*. Susan.llewelyn@hmc.ox.ac.uk.

Lorenz, K. (1935). Der Kumpan in der umwelt des vogels. Der artgenosse als auslösendes moment sozialer verhaltensweisen. *Journal für ornithologie*, *83*: 137–215, 289–413.

Lorenz, K. (1970). *Studies in Animal and Human Behaviour, Volume 1*. Cambridge, MA: Harvard University Press.

Lyons-Ruth, K., Connell, D., Grunebaum, H., & Botein, S. (1990). Infants at social risk: maternal depression and family support services as mediators of infant development and security of attachment. *Child Development*, *61*: 85–98.

Mace, C. (2004). Psychotherapy and neuroscience: how close can they get? In: J. Corrigall & H. Wilkinson (Eds.), *Revolutionary Connections. Psychotherapy and Neuroscience* (pp. 163–174). London: Karnac.

Mace, C., Beeken, S., & Embleton, J. (2006). Beginning therapy: clinical outcomes in brief treatments by psychiatric trainees. *Psychiatric Bulletin*, *30*: 7–10.

MacLean, P. D. (1970). *The Triune Brain, Emotion, and Scientific Bias*. In: F. O. Scmitt (Ed.), *The Neurosciences. Second Study Programme* (pp. 336–349). New York: Rockefeller University Press.

MacLean, P. D., Whittal, M. L., Thordarson, D. S., Taylor, S., Sochting, I., & Koch, W. J. (2001). Cognitive versus behavior therapy in the group treatment of obsessive–compulsive disorder. *Journal of Consulting and Clinical Psychology*, *69*(2): 205–214.

Madrid, A., Skolek, S., & Shapiro, F. (2006). Repairing failures in bonding through EMDR. *Clinical Case Studies*, *5*(4): 271–286.

Mallinckrodt, B., Wei, M., Larson, L. M., & Zakalik, R. A. (2005). Adult attachment, depressive symptoms, and validation from self versus others. *American Psychological Association*, *52*(3): 368–377.

McBride, C., Atkinson, L., Quilty, L. C., & Bagby, R. M. (2006). Attachment as moderator of treatment outcome in major depression: a randomized control trial of interpersonal psychotherapy versus cognitive behavior therapy. *Journal of Consulting and Clinical Psychology*, *74*(6): 1041–1054.

McDermott, I., & Jago, W. (2001). *Brief NLP Therapy*. London: Sage Publications.

McDermut, W., Miller, I. W., & Brown, R. A. (2001). The efficacy of group psychotherapy for depression: a meta-analysis and review of the empirical research. *Clinical Psychology: Science and Practice, 8*: 98–116.

Merhabian, A. (1981). *Silent Messages: Implicit Communication of Emotions and Attitudes*. Belmont, CA: Wadsworth.

Miller, G., & de Shazer, S. (2000). Emotions in solution-focused therapy: a re-examination. *Family Process, 39*(1): 5–23.

Mollon, P. (2004). *EMDR and the Energy Therapies. Psychoanalytic Perspectives*. London: Karnac.

Moorey, S. (1996). Cognitive therapy. In: W. Dryden (Ed.), *Handbook of Individual Therapy*. London: Sage.

Mortberg, E., Clark, D. M., Sundin, O., & Aberg Wistedt, A. (2007). Intensive group cognitive treatment and individual cognitive therapy vs. treatment as usual in social phobia: a randomized controlled trial. *Acta Psychiatrica Scandinavica, 115*: 142–154.

Moses, M. D. (2007). Enhancing attachments: conjoint couples therapy with EMDR. In: F. Shapiro, F. Kaslow, & L. Maxfield (Eds.), *Handbook of EMDR and Family Therapy Processes*. NJ: Wiley.

Murray, L., & Cooper, P. J. (Eds.) (1997). *Postpartum Depression and Child Development*. New York: Guilford Press.

Nardone, G., & Portelli, C. (2005). *Knowing Through Changing: The Evolution of Brief Strategic Therapy*. Carmarthen: Crown House.

Nardone, G., & Watzlawick, P. (2002). *Brief Strategic Therapy*. MD: Rowman and Littlefield.

Nardone, G., & Watzlawick, P. (2004). *The Prisons of Food: Strategic Solution-orientated Research and Treatment of Eating Disorders*. London: Karnac.

NICE (2004a). *Cognitive Behavioural Therapy*. London: Department of Health.

NICE (2004b). *Eating Disorders: Care Interventions in the Treatment and Management of Anorexia Nervosa, Bulimia Nervosa and Related Eating Disorders*. London: Department of Health.

NICE (2005). *Obsessive Compulsive Disorder - Care Interventions in the Treatment of Obsessive Compulsive Disorder and Body Dysmorphic Disorder*. London: Department of Health.

NICE (2007a). *Management of Depression in Primary and Secondary Care*. London: Department of Health.

NICE (2007b). *Anxiety. Management of Anxiety (Panic Disorder, with or without Agoraphobia and Generalised Anxiety Disorder) in Adults in Primary, Secondary and Community Care*. London: Department of Health.

NLPtCA website (2006). http://www.nlptca.com/whatisnlpt.php available on-line (accessed 19 January 2008).

Norcross, J. C. (Ed.) (2002). *Psychotherapy Relationships that Work: Therapist Contributions and Responsiveness to Patient Needs*. New York: Oxford University Press.

O'Hanlon, B. (2000). *Do One Thing Different*. New York: Harper Collins.

O'Hanlon, B. (2003). *A Guide to Inclusive Therapy*. New York: W. W. Norton.

O'Hanlon, B., & Bertolino, B. (1998). *Even From a Broken Web. Brief, Respectful Solution-Oriented Therapy for Sexual Abuse and Trauma*. New York: W. W. Norton.

O'Hanlon, B., & Weiner-Davis, M. (2003). *In Search of Solutions. A New Direction in Psychotherapy*. New York: W. W. Norton.

O'Hanlon, W. H. (1987). *Taproots:Underlying Principles of Milton Erickson's Therapy and Hypnosis*. New York: W. W. Norton.

Ost, L. G. (1996). Long-term effects of behavior therapy for specific phobia. In: M. R. Mavissakalian & R. F. Prien (Eds.), *Long-term Treatments for Anxiety Disorders* (pp. 121–170). Washington, DC: American Psychiatric Press.

Ost, L. G., Fellenius, J., & Sterner, U. (1991). Applied tension, exposure in vivo, and tension only in the treatment of blood phobia. *Behaviour Research and Therapy, 29*: 561–575.

Panksepp, J. (1998). *Affective Neuroscience: The Foundations of Human and Animal Emotions*. Oxford: Oxford University Press.

Pavlov, I. P. (1927) [1904]. *Conditioned Reflexes*. London: Routledge.

Paykel, R., Scott, J., & Teasdale, J. D. (1999). Prevention of relapse by cognitive therapy in residual depression: a controlled trial. *Archives of General Psychiatry, 56*: 829–835.

Perls, F., Hefferline, F., & Goodman, P. (1973) [1951]. *Gestalt Therapy. Excitement & Growth in the Human Personality*. New York: Julian Press Dell.

Perry, B. D., Pollard, R. A., Blakely, T. L., Baker, W. L., & Vigilante, D. (1995). Childhood trauma, the neurobiology of adaptation, and "use-dependent" development of the brain. How "states" become "traits". *Infant Mental Health Journal, 16*: 271–291.

Pert, C. (1997). *Molecules of Emotion. Why You Feel the Way You Feel.* London: Pocket Books.

Radke-Yarrow, M., Cummings, E., Kuczynski, L., & Chapman, M. (1985). Patterns of Attachment in two and three year olds in normal families and families with parental depression. *Child Development, 56*: 884–893.

Rizzolatti, G., Fadiga, L., Fogassi, L., & Gallese, V. (1999). Resonance behaviours and mirror neurons. *Archives of Italian Biology, 137*: 85–100.

Rogers, A., Oliver, D., Bower, P., Lovell, K., & Richards, D. A. (2004). People's understandings of using a self-help clinic: implications for integration and effectiveness in primary care. *Patient Education and Counselling, 53*: 41–46.

Rogers, C. R. (1951). *Client Centred Therapy.* London: Constable.

Rosen, S. (1992). *My Voice Will Go With You. The Teaching Tales of Milton H. Erickson.* New York: W. W. Norton.

Roth, A., & Fonagy, P. (2005). *What Works for Whom: A Critical Review of Psychotherapy Research* (2nd edn). London: Guilford Press.

Rothschild, B. (2000). *The Body Remembers. The Psychophysiology of Trauma and Trauma Treatment.* New York: W. W. Norton.

Ryle, A. (1990). *Cognitive Analytic Therapy: Active Participation in Change.* Chichester: Wiley & Sons.

Ryle, A. (1995a). *Cognitive Analytic Therapy: Developments in Theory and Practice.* Chichester: Wiley & Sons.

Ryle, A. (1995b). Transference and counter-transference variations in the course of the cognitive–analytic therapy of two borderline patients: the relation to the diagrammatic reformulation of self-states. *British Journal of Medical Psychology, 68*: 109–124.

Ryle, A., & Beard, H. (1993). The integrative effect of reformulation: cognitive analytic therapy with a patient with borderline personality disorder. *British Journal of Medical Psychology, 66*: 249–258.

Satir, V. (1972). *Peoplemaking.* Palo Alto, CA: Science and Behaviour Books.

Schore, A. N. (1994). *Affect Regulation and the Origin of the Self: The Neurobiology of Emotional Development.* Mahwah, NJ. Lawrence Erlbaum.

Schore, A. N. (2003a). *Affect Regulation and the Repair of the Self.* London: W. W. Norton.

Schore, A. N. (2003b). *Affect Dysregulation and the Disorders of the Self.* London: W. W. Norton.

Scott, J., Teasdale, J. D., & Paykel, E. S. (2000). Effects of cognitive therapy on psychosocial symptoms and social functioning in residual depression. *British Journal of Psychiatry, 177*: 440–446.

Shapiro, F. (1989). Efficacy of the eye movement desensitization procedure in the treatment of traumatic memories. *Journal of Traumatic Stress, 2*: 199–223.

Shapiro, F. (2001). *Eye Movement Desensitization and Reprocessing: Basic Principles, Protocols and Procedures* (2nd edn). New York: Guilford Press.

Shapiro, F. (2002). EMDR as an integrative psychotherapy approach: experts of diverse orientation explore the paradigm prism. In: F. Shapiro, F. Kaslow, & L. Maxfield (Eds.), *Handbook of EMDR and Family Therapy Processes*. New York: Wiley.

Shapiro, F., & Brown, S. (2006). EMDR in the treatment of borderline personality disorder. *Clinical Case Studies, 5*(5): 403–420.

Shaver, P. R., Belsky, J., & Brennan, K. A. (2000). The adult attachment interview and self-reports of romantic attachment: associations across domains and methods. *Personal Relationships, 7*: 25–43.

Shepherd, J., Stein, K., & Milne, R. (2000). Eye movement desentitization and reprocessing in the treatment of post-traumatic stress disorder: a review of an emerging therapy. *Psychological Medicine, 30*(4): 863–871.

Short, D., Erickson, B. A., & Erickson Klein, R. (2005). *Hope and Resiliency: Understanding the Psychotherapeutic Strategies of Milton H. Erickson*. Carmarthen, Wales: Crown House.

Showers, C. J., & Kevlyn, S. B. (1999). Organization of knowledge about a relationship partner: implications for liking and loving. *Journal of Interpersonal Relations and Group Processes, 76*(6): 958–971.

Siegel, D. J. (1999). *Developing Mind: Toward a Neurobiology of Interpersonal Experience*. New York: Guilford Press.

Simpkins, C. A., & Simpkins, A. M. (2008). An exploratory outcome comparison between an Ericksonian approach to therapy and brief dynamic therapy. *American Journal of Clinical Hypnosis, 50*(3): 217–232.

Sinason, V. (Ed.) (2002). *Attachment, Trauma and Multiplicity. Working with Dissociative Identity Disorder*. Hove: Brunner Routledge.

Siqueland, L., Rynn, M., & Diamond, G. S. (2005). Cognitive behavioral and attachment based family therapy for anxious adolescents: Phase I and II studies. *Journal of Anxiety Disorders, 19*(4): 361–381.

Skinner, B. F. (1938). *The Behaviour of Organisms*. New York: Appleton-Century-Crofts.

Skinner, B. F. (1961). Teaching machines. *Scientific American, 205*(5): 90–107.

Soberman, G. B., Greenwald, R., & Rule, D. L. (2002). A controlled study of eye movement desensitization and reprocessing (EMDR) for boys with conduct problems. *Journal of Aggression, Maltreatment, and Trauma, 6*: 217–236.

Solms, M. (1996). Towards an anatomy of the unconscious. *Journal of Clinical Psychoanalysis, 5*: 331–367.

SPeDi Trial (Sheffield Personality Disorders) (2007). www.shef.ac.uk/spedi/.

Stams, G. J., Dekovic, M., Buist, K., & de Vries, L. (2006). Effectiviteit van oplossingsgerichte korte therapie: een meta-analyse (Efficacy of solution focused brief therapy: a meta-analysis). *Gedragstherapie, 39*(2): 81–95.

Stangier, U., Heidenreich, T., Peitz, M., Lauterbach, W., & Clark, D. M. (2003). Cognitive therapy for social phobia: individual versus group treatment. *Behaviour Research & Therapy, 41*(9): 991–1007.

Stern, N. (1998). *The Motherhood Constellation. A Unified View of Parent–Infant Psychotherapy*. London: Karnac.

Stiles, W. B., Barkham, M., Twigg, E., Mellor-Clark, J., & Cooper, M. (2006). Effectiveness of Cognitive-behavioural, person-centred and psychodynamic therapies as practised in UK National Health Service settings. *Psychological Medicine, 36*: 555–566.

Stiles, W. B., Shapiro, D. A., & Elliott, R. (1986). Are all psychotherapies equivalent? *American Psychologist, 41*: 165–180.

Teasdale, J. D. (1999). Emotional processing, three modes of mind and the prevention of relapse in depression. *Behaviour Research and Therapy, 37*(Suppl. 1): S53–S57.

Thom, A., Sartory, G., & Johren, P. (2000). Comparison between one-session psychological treatment and benzodiazepine in dental phobia. *Journal of Consulting & Clinical Psychology, 68*: 378–387.

Thorndike, E. L. (1913). *Educational Psychology*. New York: Columbia University Press.

Van der Kolk, B. A. (2005). Developmental trauma disorder. *Psychiatric Annals, 35*(5): 401–408.

Van der Kolk, B. A. (2006). Clinical implications of neuroscience research in PTSD. *Annals of the New York Academy of Science, xxxx*: 1–17.

Van der Kolk, B. A., Rauch, S. L., Fisler, R. E., Albert, N. M., Orr, S. P., Savage, C. R., Fischman, A. G., Jenike, M. A., & Pitman, R. K. (1996). A symptom provocation study of post-traumatic stress disorder using positron emission tomography and script driven imagery. *Archives of General Psychiatry*, 53: 380–387.

Van Etten, M. L., & Taylor, S. (1998). Comparative efficacy of treatments for post-traumatic stress disorder: a meta-analysis. *Clinical Psychology and Psychotherapy*, 5: 126–144.

Visser, S., & Bouman, T. K. (2001). The treatment of hypochondriasis: exposure plus response prevention vs cognitive therapy. *Behaviour Research and Therapy*, 39: 423–442.

Wake, L. (2008). *Neurolinguistic Psychotherapy: A Postmodern Approach.* London: Routledge.

Warwick, H. M. C., Clark, D. M., & Cobb, A. M. (1996). A controlled trial of cognitive–behavioural treatment of hypochondriasis. *British Journal of Psychiatry*, 169: 189–195.

Watson, J. B., & Rayner, R. (1920). Conditioned emotional reactions. *Journal of Experimental Psychology*, 3: 1–14.

Watzlawick, P. (1978). *The Language of Change. Elements of Therapeutic Communication.* New York: W. W. Norton.

Watzlawick, P., Weakland, J., & Fisch, R. (1974). *Change: Principles of Problem Formation and Problem Resolution.* New York: W. W. Norton.

Westbrook, D., & Kirk, J. (2005). The clinical effectiveness of cognitive behavioural therapy: outcome for a large sample of adults treated in routine practice. *Behaviour Research and Therapy*, 43: 1243–1261.

Westen, D. (1995). Social cognition and object relations scale: Q-sort for projective stories (SCORS-Q), unpublished manuscript.

Whitfield, G., & Williams, C. (2003). The evidence base for cognitive-behavioural therapy in depression: delivery in busy clinical settings. *Advances in Psychiatric Treatment*, 9: 21–30.

Whittal, M. L., Thordarson, D. S., & MacLean, P. D. (2005). Treatment of obsessive-compulsive disorder: cognitive behavior therapy vs. exposure and response prevention. *Behavior Research Therapy*, 43(12): 1559–1576.

Winnicott, D. (1960). Ego distortion in terms of the true and false self. In: *The Maturational Processes and the Facilitating Environment.* London: Hogarth.

Winnicott, D. (1971). Transitional objects and transitional phenomena. In: *Playing and Reality.* London: Tavistock.

Young, J. E. (1990). *Cognitive Therapy for Personality Disorders: A Schema-focussed Approach.* Sarasota: Professional Resource Exchange.

Zeig, J. (1980). *A Teaching Seminar with Milton H. Erickson.* New York: Brunner Mazel.

Zeig, J. (1985). *Experiencing Erickson: An Introduction to the Man and His Work.* New York: Brunner Mazel.

INDEX